RECIPES FROM AN INDIAN KITCHEN

RECIPES FROM AN
INDIAN
KITCHEN

AUTHENTIC RECIPES FROM ACROSS INDIA

This edition published by Parragon Books Ltd in 2015 and distributed by

Parragon Inc.
440 Park Avenue South, 13th Floor
New York, NY 10016
www.parragon.com/lovefood

ISBN 978-1-4723-9320-3

Printed in China

New recipes by Sunil Vijayakar
Introduction by Manju Malhi
Recipe photography by Mike Cooper
Home economy by Lincoln Jefferson
Designed by Geoff Borin

Notes for the Reader
This book uses standard kitchen measuring spoons and cups. All spoon and cup measurements are level unless otherwise indicated. Unless otherwise stated, milk is assumed to be whole, eggs are large, individual vegetables are medium, pepper is freshly ground black pepper. Unless otherwise stated, all root vegetables should be peeled prior to using.

The times given are an approximate guide only. Preparation times differ according to the techniques used by different people, and the cooking times may also vary from those given.

For best results, use a food thermometer when cooking meat. Check the latest government guidelines for current advice.

Vegetarians should be aware that some of the prepared ingredients used in the recipes in this book might contain animal products. Always check the package before use.

Picture acknowledgments
The publisher would like to thank Getty Images Ltd for permission to reproduce copyright material on the following pages:
2, 6, 10–11, 12 (t), 13 (b), 14 (t), 15 (b), 16, 18–19, 24–25, 30 (t, cl & cr), 31, 38–39 (all), 52 (t & b), 53, 60–61, 74–75 (all), 90 (t, bl & br), 91, 98–99, 122, 123, 142–143, 150 (t & b), 151, 164–165, 174 (tl, tr & b), 175, 186–187, 198 (tl, tr & b), 199 & 210–211.

CONTENTS

INTRODUCTION

The Indian kitchen is not only the focal point for cooking but also the essential hub of the home where family members can come together. It has long been the Indian woman's domain—responsible for keeping it pristine and in working order, she has taken pride of place in the one room where her rules have reigned for decades.

Traditionally, her day would begin early. She would bathe before entering the kitchen because this room would be considered sacred. She would offer a prayer to the gods and light incense, whose heady fragrance would suffuse the fresh morning air. The water would be boiling in a stainless-steel vessel on a customary Indian stove (*chulha*). She would take out a box of tea leaves, which she would store in her Aladdin's cave of ingredients along with an array of spices, pickles, nuts, rice, and flours. Then the preparation of the first meal of the day would begin. It could be an assortment of dishes—ranging from freshly cooked breads and pancakes to eggs and Indian confections—for the family to eat at home or to be packed up, ready to go when they head out, either to school or work. The menus for the meals for the rest of the day would have already been planned in advance, depending on the availability of seasonal ingredients. All meals in India are given equal importance, and lunch is served with as much attention to detail and effort as supper time, which then offers another elaborate spread of sweet and savory snacks and appetizers (*namkeen*). However, the most engaging meal of the day would have to be dinnertime, which is late in the day, when the family shares the day's experiences and catches up on news. The dinner setting can consist of two or three vegetable dishes along with freshly made chapatis and rice. Just before bedtime, hot milk flavored with sugar and often cardamom would is drunk, not only by the children but also by the adults of the house.

In modern India, the role of the kitchen has changed dramatically to suit the needs of a dynamic lifestyle in a fast-paced society. The urban areas of the world's largest democracy find professional men and women skipping many traditional practices, including breakfast, to save time and to meet the demands of their jobs. This has created a new style of eating, be it in the home or outside, and has evolved into innovative meals.

BRIEF HISTORY OF
INDIAN CUISINE

The Indian food we know today is steeped in a rich culinary history. It is accepted by many that the origins of Indian history and civilization are as old as humankind itself. Evidence of one of the earliest civilizations in the world, known as the Harappan civilization, dating back to around 2500 BC, can be found at a site called Mohenjodaro in southern Pakistan, formerly part of India. Animal bones found at Mohenjodaro indicate that meat was eaten. Settlers started to farm, which led to the discovery of grains such as wheat and barley. Legumes such as lentils and rice also became a staple food in their diet. Ancient tandoor ovens have been found at the archeological site, meaning that baking was popular. Also found was proof of objects that could only have come from the Middle East region, indicating the first movement of outsiders into the country. With extensive trade both by land and sea to the Indus Valley cities, the exchange of foods, seeds, and plants, became one of the first external influences. This was called the Indus Valley Civilization.

Life appeared to be stable until around 1600 BC, when order began to decline, and a new wave of people, known as Aryans, entered India from central Asia. They were a semi-nomadic race who wandered with herds of cattle. Gradually, they evolved into a more settled society and it is thought that around 1000 BC the roots of Hinduism were shaped. This led to the development of the Hindu caste system dividing food habits of people by caste. And among this rigid tier system of classes, determined by heredity, the Brahmins or priests at the top were vegetarians, while the Kshatriyas or warriors ate meat. Half a century later, around the time of the birth of Lord Buddha, a new religion or philosophy of Buddhism began to be practiced and Jainism was also emerging. The latter had a marked influence on the cuisine. Jains are strong believers in nonviolence, and their food, apart from being cooked without meat, is also cooked without onions and garlic or any other root vegetable that might kill insects or other animals living in the soil.

By far the biggest external influence on Indian cuisine would have to be the religious faith of Islam. From about 700 AD, India was invaded by Arab Muslims and, for the next two centuries, a magnificent superpower of that period, commonly known as the Mogul Empire, was established. At the turn of the thirteenth century, they made India their home and remained at the helm of power for more than 500 years, up until the early 1800s. Mogul culture had a lasting impact on the cuisine of India, thus shaping and changing the face of Indian gastronomy. It is the kind of cuisine that people now tend to associate with India. The rulers saw food as an art form, with recipes containing as many as 25 spices delicately cooked and blended, yet each dish by itself was just a small part of an opulent, lavish feast with endless courses. The Mogul Empire introduced rose water, nuts, dried fruits, saffron, dairy products (milk, cream, butter, and yogurt), and the *dum* style of cooking dishes in a sealed vessel. One of the Mogul dynasties to invade India was the Sultan dynasty in Hyderabad, in southern India, where these culinary influences emanated into the regions, culminating in extravagant rice dishes (biryanis).

The people living in India, regardless of their own religion, tend to celebrate all religious festivals and their culinary traditions; for example, Muslims celebrate Diwali (the Hindu festival of light) while Christians take part in Eid. The majority of festivals observed in India are associated with specific regional cuisines. Although India is famed for its curries, most festivals revolve around the unifying love of sugary treats, and almost everyone is allowed to forget their culinary inhibitions and enjoy these treats to the fullest. Many of the desserts are prepared with nuts, rice, lentils, wheat, sugar, cardamom, and saffron. The largest festival in India is Diwali, around October–November, when many recipes found in Mogul cooking are adopted to make elaborate feasts.

The cuisine of Goa in western India is influenced by the Portuguese style of cooking, using European ingredients. The Portuguese, led by Vasco da Gama, started the eventual colonization of India in the fifteenth century, only to be overtaken by the British, who ruled the subcontinent from the eighteenth century onward. It would be fair to say that the British love affair with "curry" blossomed, and resulted in, among other things, the emergence of Anglo-Indian cuisine and typical Raj traditions, such as "high tea." When British rule over India ended in 1947, the subcontinent was divided into two countries— India and Pakistan, which at the time included part of what later would become Bangladesh. The resulting movement of people within the subcontinent, and consequently the migration of various regional cultures to Europe, Asia, and the Americas, meant that their distinct cooking styles inevitably merged, resulting in today's Indian cuisine ranging from Mughlai (Mogul cuisine) to Anglo-Indian to modern Chinese-influenced Indian food.

Many Indian dishes may have evolved from the principles of Ayurveda, a holistic approach to food and its preparation based around balancing the six tastes of sweet, sour, salty, pungent, bitter, and astringent.

REGIONAL CUISINE

NORTH

Lamayuru monastery at sunrise, Jammu and Kashmir

Around the world, many menus from Indian restaurants include dishes from the north of India. The north is the home of the tandoor and tandoori cooking, where food is cooked in a clay oven at extremely high temperatures. People of the north have hearty appetites and love to indulge. The curries are predominantly thick, rich, and often have creamy sauces, and they are served with breads. With the northern states of Punjab and Haryana considered India's breadbasket, rotis, parathas (flaky bread), naans (tandoor-baked leavened bread), and other wheat-base preparations are more popular than rice. However, the Himalayas are close to Jammu and Kashmir and provide the water to grow the basmati rice that is exported abroad. With particularly hot summers and severely cold winters, the north of India grows a wide mixture of fruits and vegetables, such as apples from the state of Himachal Pradesh; cauliflower from Madhya Pradesh; as well as okra; mustard; and spinach greens. The Indian state of Punjab is known for its rich dishes using dairy products, such as ghee (clarified butter), paneer (Indian cheese), milk, and cream, and nuts and dried fruits. Meat dishes reflect Mogul and Kashmiri styles of cuisine, with the creation of rich pilafs and biryanis. Notable popular dishes from the north of India include mattar paneer (peas and cheese), chicken tikka, butter chicken, fish Amritsari, meat kabobs, samosas, and dal makhani (buttery lentils), made predominantly using cumin, coriander, dried red chiles, cardamom, cinnamon, cloves, and the spice blend garam masala. Dishes are cooked in vegetable and peanut oil, with ghee being used on special occasions.

Spiced chickpea flour flatbreads (besan ki roti), p. 193

The south of India has a hot and humid climate and its states are surrounded by three bodies of water—the Arabian Sea on the west, the Bay of Bengal on the eastern side, and the Indian Ocean toward the southern side—making all the states in the south coastal. Because of its geographical location, seafood is high on the menu. Rainfall is abundant, so the supply of fresh fruit, vegetables, and rice is ample. The cuisines of the states of Karnataka, Kerala, Tamil Nadu, and Andhra Pradesh encompass the south. These regions are famed for their spices, such as peppercorns, cloves, cardamom, ginger, and cinnamon. In the state of Andhra Pradesh, the food is heavily influenced by the legacy of the Mogul Empire. Hyderabad, the capital of Andhra Pradesh, was ruled by the Nizams during the eighteenth century, when the food was shaped by Turkish, Arabic, and Irani tastes. This culminated in dishes such as the Hyderabadi biryani (baked lamb with rice) and haleem (a ground meat and wheat porridge). The state of Kerala, known as the land of coconuts, specializes in Malabari cuisine, using seafood combined with fresh spices, such as curry leaves, mustard seeds, and asafetida, along with tamarind and coconut to create sumptuous fish curries. The state is also known for its vegetarian traditional banquet, known as *sadya*,

comprising of boiled rice served with a selection of side dishes made with vegetables and lentils and a sweet preparation called *payasam*. Recipes from Tamil Nadu make abundant use of chiles; this style of cooking is known as Chettinad cuisine. Tamil Nadu is also celebrated for its dosas and idlis. Dosas are pancakes made from a batter of fermented lentils and rice, commonly accompanied by sambhar (a spicy vegetable and lentil dish) and coconut- and chile-base chutneys. Idlis are made from the same ingredients as dosas but are steamed instead of fried. Despite India being one of the largest tea-growers in the world, south Indians are staunch coffee drinkers and Mysore coffee is their favorite afternoon drink.

Peppered south Indian chicken curry (murgh chettinad), p. 129

SOUTH

The Kerala backwaters

EAST

Trams, buses, and traffic, Kolkata

Of all the regions of India, the heaviest rainfall is in the east of the country, so rice grown in the vast paddy fields is the staple of the people of the states of West Bengal, Orissa, Sikkim, Nagaland, Assam, Manipur, Arunachal Pradesh, Meghalaya, Mizoram, and Tripura. The cuisine of these regions is strongly influenced by Chinese and Mongolian cooking styles, so the preparations are simple, with uncomplicated flavors, and the steaming of food is preferred to frying. The people of West Bengal are known for their sweet tooth, which means that some of India's most sought-after desserts (confections created with dairy products, nuts, and spices) come from Kolkata. Near the coastal regions of eastern India, fish is prepared in oil and cooked with a spice blend known as *panch phoran* (Bengali five-spice seasoning). The five spices in panch phoran are cumin seeds, onion or nigella seeds, mustard seeds, fennel seeds, and fenugreek seeds. East Indians inland favor beef and pork as their nonvegetarian fare. Sikkim and its surrounding states in the east have adopted the food culture of neighboring countries, such as Tibet, with the creation of *thukpa* (a clear noodle-base broth) and *momos* (steamed dumplings made with ground chicken or mutton), which have grown to be a popular street food and are served with a red chili sauce dip.

Steamed chicken dumplings (murgh momo), p. 89

Vegetable noodle broth (thukpa), p. 92

The diets of people in the west of India are largely based on Hinduism and are predominantly vegetarian, particularly in the state of Gujarat. Their snacks, known as *farsan*, are legendary and include a huge selection of rice and chickpea flour treats that are sold all over India. Similar to Kerala, Gujarat has its own style of *thali*, serving ten vegetarian dishes on one plate. The food of Rajasthan includes meat dishes, such as *laal maas*, which literally means "red meat"—the color red indicates the amount of chile that would be used to prepare this recipe. There's also a dish that would be fair to say is an acquired taste called *dal baati churma*—a combination of lentils (dal), wheat flour dough balls (baati), and a sugar-and-wheat flour mixture (churma) cooked in clarified butter. The dry, arid, and desert climate of Rajasthan means that there is a relatively small variety of vegetables available, so preserving them as pickles (*aachar*) and chutneys is common, and lentils are cooked daily. Maharashtra is the state in which the commercial hub of Mumbai is located. Street food is synonymous with this city, and pomfret, a popular flat fish with a distinctive flavor, is cooked in a variety of ways. Peanuts and coconut are widely available and used liberally in curries, relishes, and confections. Malvani and Konkan cuisines make the most

of coconuts and fish seasoned with a sour-tasting, deep-purple berry called *kokum* (mangosteen). Goa—with its lush, green coastline—makes use of fresh fish and is also influenced by the legacy left by the Portuguese in dishes such as vindaloo (a fiery curry made with garlic and vinegar) and *xacuti* (a thick chicken and coconut curry with dried red chiles) served with European bread rolls. Many of the flavors of Goan cuisine are rich and piquant and run through its cooked meats, such as Goan spicy pork sausages (*chouricos*), which are eaten by the large Catholic community.

Goan spiced chicken (murgh xacuti), p. 137

WEST

Victoria or Chhatrapati Shivaji Terminus, Mumbai

EATING INDIAN STYLE

Generally, in Indian cuisine, there is only one course and all the dishes are served together, including any soups, but Indian restaurants throughout the world often divide dishes into appetizers, main dishes with sides, and desserts to make an Indian meal more familiar to eating habits in the Western world. What many consider as Indian appetizers, such as the deep-fried snacks samosas and onion bhajis, are actually commonly served with tea in India, while desserts or sweet dishes are eaten during festivals. The traditional way of serving Indian food is on a *thali*, which is a large, stainless-steel tray-like plate. The *thali* may contain small, stainless-steel bowls (*katoris*) in which are placed various vegetable and lentil preparations, including relishes, while rice and bread (roti or pooris) are served in the center of the thali. In the west and south of India, it is not uncommon to see food being served on glossy green banana leaves.

Traditionally there are no eating implements, such as knives or forks, and the food is eaten only with the right hand because the left hand is regarded as the hand that is used only for personal cleaning. It is, therefore, essential to wash one's hands before eating. A portion of the bread or roti is torn and used as a scoop to gather and scoop up a quantity of an accompanying dish. Rice acts as a base for many Indian meals and only one dish is sampled with every mouthful of rice in order to fully appreciate the individual flavors and spice notes of every dish. Drinking beverages during an Indian meal is a fairly new phenomenon and, like the rice, the drink served needs to be neutral, such as water. However, many Indian meals are now served with sweet drinks, such as rose syrup beverages, beer, or lager. And although certain tannins may affect the flavor of Indian foods, there are now wines that have been created to match the spices.

It would not make sense to use authentic Indian cookware and utensils that were used a century ago, because they have been replaced by better, more efficient, and practical kitchen equipment. So here is a list of items that would be worth stocking for everyday Indian cooking:

- KARAHI (Indian wok) or a large, heavy saucepan for frying foods

- TAWA or a flat, heavy griddle or skillet for the preparation of rotis and pancakes

- ROLLING PIN for shaping rotis and other breads

- MEASURING SPOONS for accurate measurement of spices

- MEASURING CUPS to make sure the ingredients are the right quantities for the right balance of spices

- SMALL SKILLET with a heavy base for dry-roasting spices in small batches

- METAL TONGS to turn breads and other hot foods

- STEAMER suitable for the preparation of south Indian dishes

- FOOD PROCESSOR to assist in chopping and blending ingredients

- MORTAR AND PESTLE for coarsely grinding spices

- SPICE GRINDER for preparing fresh spice blends

- PRESSURE COOKER for cooking dried beans and other legumes that would otherwise take hours to cook

ESSENTIAL EQUIPMENT FOR INDIAN COOKING

GLOSSARY OF INGREDIENTS

Look for Indian ingredients in the specialty sections of supermarkets. More unusual ones are available in Indian or Asian grocery stores or online.

Asafetida
This finely ground resin is known as "the devil's dung," because its pungent, sulfurous aroma is especially off-putting until cooked. Asafetida is used only in small amounts and it is sold in block or powder form. You could use garlic powder instead.

Banana leaves
South Indian food is often served on these large, glossy, dark-green leaves. They can also be wrapped around food before cooking to seal in the flavors.

Basmati rice
Grown in the foothills of the Himalayas, this long-grained rice is valued for its delicate fragrance and silky grains that separate during cooking. Outside of India, basmati rice is synonymous with Indian food, but more than 20 varieties of rice are grown and used within India. Consequently, basmati is often saved for special occasions and celebrations.

Bay leaves
Bay leaves used in Indian cuisine are different from those used in the West. Asian bay leaves come from the cassis tree, whereas Western ones are obtained from sweet bay laurel. However, Western bay leaves are fine to use if you cannot obtain Asian ones

Cardamom
Known as the "queen of spices" (black pepper is the "king"), green cardamom is one of the most popular flavorings in Indian cooking, used in both savory and sweet dishes as well as in drinks. Although the whole pods are often used in recipes, they're not meant to be eaten, so be careful to remove them from the finished dish before serving. Black cardamom has a much heavier, pronounced flavor and is only used in savory recipes. Ground cardamom is available, but grinding small quantities of the seeds at home will produce a better flavor.

Chiles, fresh
Synonymous as chiles are with Indian food, they are relative newcomers to the Indian spice box, having been introduced by the Portuguese. Unfortunately, it is difficult to tell how hot a chile is by appearance alone. As a general rule, the small, thin ones are hot, while the large, fleshy ones tend to be milder. Most of the heat is in the seeds and membranes, so it is best to remove them if you prefer a milder flavor.

Chili powder
When fresh green chiles are ripe, they turn a rich red. These are dried to obtain dried red chiles. Chili powder is made by finely grinding dried red chiles. Look for bright-red Kashmiri chili powder, made from the chiles that grow in the northern region of Kashmir.

Cinnamon

One of the oldest spices, cinnamon is obtained from the rolled, dried bark of a tropical plant related to the laurel family. It has a warm flavor and is used in both savory and sweet dishes.

Cloves

Frequently used whole or ground in Indian cooking, these dried flower buds have a strong, aromatic flavor that can be overpowering if used in abundance or chewed.

Coconut

Considered the "fruit of the gods," coconuts are important in Hindu religious ceremonies, as well as to the kitchens of southern India and Goa. The creamy, white flesh and thin, cloudy coconut water are used in cooking and as snacks. Coconut milk is made by grating, blending, and squeezing the juice from the coconut flesh. Different grades of thickness exist; the first extraction is thicker and the second, made from soaking the remaining blended coconut in water, is thinner. Coconut cream is richer and thicker than coconut milk, with a higher ratio of coconut to water. Both are available in cans or cartons, but you will may need to get coconut cream (which is not the same as sweetened cream of coconut used for beverages) from an Indian or Asian grocery store or online.

Coriander and cilantro

Fresh cilantro leaves from the coriander plant add a tangy, citrus flavor and a splash of vibrant green to many Indian dishes. The round seeds from the same plant—with their sweet, mellow flavor—taste very different from the leaves. They are sold as seeds or a ground powder.

Cumin

Popular with cooks in all regions of India, cumin is prized for its distinctive, strong flavor and digestive qualities. The thin, slightly elongated seeds are available in two varieties: brown and black. Each has its own distinctive flavor and one cannot be substituted for the other. Cumin is used either whole or ground.

Curry leaves

A hallmark of southern cooking, these have an assertive flavor. Fresh and dried versions are available. Dried ones can be stored in an airtight container and fresh ones can be frozen and used as and when required.

Dried mango powder (amchoor)

This is made from unripe green mangoes that are dried and ground to form a powder. It is used as a meat tenderizer, as well as in dishes that require a sour flavor.

Fennel seeds

These have a taste similar to that of aniseed. The seeds range in color from bright green to pale green and tan and resemble a ridged grain of rice. Fennel seeds are used extensively in Indian cooking and are an essential ingredient in some key spice mixes (masalas), such as panch phoran. In India, fennel seeds are chewed as an after-dinner breath freshener.

Fenugreek

A strong and aromatic herb, fenugreek is cultivated in India and Pakistan but is native to the Mediterranean region. The fresh leaves are cooked like spinach, and they are also dried and used in smaller quantities to flavor meat and poultry dishes. The small, irregularly shaped fenugreek seeds have a distinctive flavor and a powerful taste. They are also available in ground form.

Garam masala

The word *garam* means "heat," and *masala* is an Indian term for "spice mix." The basic ingredients are cinnamon, cardamom, cloves, and black pepper, a blend of spices believed to create body heat. Ground garam masala is usually added toward the end of cooking, whereas whole garam masala is added to the cooking fat at the start of cooking.

Garlic
Fresh garlic is an integral part of Asian cooking. It is always used crushed, finely chopped, or made into a paste.

Ghee
Ghee is an Indian form of clarified butter. The traditional rich flavor of many Indian dishes, especially those from the northern regions, comes, at least in part, from cooking with ghee. Ghee can be heated to a high temperature without burning, but its high cholesterol content means that it is slowly being replaced on an everyday basis with vegetable oils.

Ginger
Like garlic, ginger adds an authentic flavor to Indian cooking. This knobbly rhizome imparts a warm, spicy taste to a wide variety of meat, poultry, fish, and vegetarian dishes. For the best flavor, buy fresh ginger with a tight, smooth skin; a wrinkled skin is an indication that the flesh is drying out.

Lentils, beans, and peas
Dal is the word Indians use to describe legumes, such as split dried lentils, beans, and peas, as well as the many dishes prepared with these ingredients. Dals are a daily feature of menus across India and provide the backbone of most vegetarian meals.

Mint
Introduced to India by the Persians, this fresh-tasting herb is particularly popular in northern India, where it garnishes rich meat and poultry dishes. Fresh mint also features in many chutneys, raitas, and drinks.

Mustard seeds
Tiny, round mustard seeds are used in cooking throughout India. Black and brown are the most common varieties and can be used interchangeably. They lend a nutty flavor to a dish. White mustard seeds are usually reserved for making pickles.

Nigella seeds
These tiny, black seeds are also known as black onion or kalonji seeds, although they have nothing to do with onions. Their flavor is nutty and peppery. They are used whole for flavoring vegetables, pickles, breads, and snacks.

Palm sugar
This dark, coarse, and unrefined sugar, sometimes referred to as jaggery, is made from the sap of the coconut palm tree. It usually comes in the form of a solid cake in a cone or barrel shape.

Panch phoran
Panch phoran is a Bengali spice mixture made up of equal quantities of fenugreek seeds, fennel seeds, mustard seeds, nigella seeds, and cumin seeds.

Paneer
For India's millions of vegetarians, this firm, white cheese is a source of daily protein. Although paneer has a bland flavor, it readily absorbs flavors when cooked with other ingredients, and its firm texture means that it is ideal for broiling, grilling, and roasting. Paneer is sold in Asian grocery stores, but it is simple to make at home (see recipe on page 28).

Peppercorns
Fresh green berries are dried in the sun to obtain black pepper. Green berries come from the pepper vine native to the monsoon forests of southwest India. Black peppercorns will keep well in an airtight jar, but ground black pepper loses its wonderful aromatic flavor quickly; it is best to grind peppercorns as needed.

Poppy seeds
The opium poppy, grown mainly in the tropics, produces the best poppy seeds. There are two

varieties: white and black. The white seeds are ground and added to dishes to give them a nutty flavor. They are also used as a thickener and as a topping for naan.

Rose water
Rose water is the diluted extract of a special strain of edible rose, the petals of which are often used to garnish Mogul dishes. Rose syrup, used in beverages and desserts, is made from rose water, sugar, and water.

Saffron
The most expensive spice in the world, these thin threads come from the dried stamens of the crocus flower. It is so costly because the stamens are hand-picked and around 250,000 stamens are needed to produce just 1 pound of saffron. Indian saffron is grown in Kashmir and is used to add a vibrant gold color and a distinctive, slightly musky taste to many Indian dishes.

Silver foil [varak]
Indian desserts and sweets are elevated to special status with a decoration of edible silver (or gold) dust pressed onto delicate, ultra-thin sheets.

Tamarind
Resembling pea pods at first, tamarind turns dark brown with a thin, hard outer shell when ripe. The flesh is sold dried and has to be soaked in hot water to yield a pulp. Ready-to-use tamarind paste is available from Asian grocery stores. Valued for its distinctive and pronounced sour flavor, tamarind is added to many fish and vegetable dishes.

Turmeric
The instant sunshine of many Indian dishes, fresh turmeric rhizomes resemble fresh ginger and have a beige-brown skin and bright-yellow flesh. Fresh turmeric is dried and ground to produce this essential spice, which should be used in carefully measured quantities to prevent a bitter taste.

Yogurt
There are countless uses for yogurt in the Indian kitchen. It is used as a meat tenderizer and a souring agent, as well as being the main ingredient in numerous raitas and some chutneys. Indian yogurt, often referred to as "curd," is made from buffalo milk. Regular plain yogurt, whisked until smooth, is a good substitute.

BASIC RECIPES

GINGER PASTE

1 large root of fresh ginger

vegetable oil, as needed

1 Use a vegetable peeler to peel the ginger or scrape off the skin with a small, sharp knife.

2 Coarsely chop the ginger and put it into a blender or food processor and process to a puree, adding enough vegetable oil to enable the blades to move. Transfer to an airtight container and store in the refrigerator for 6–8 weeks or freeze in small quantities and defrost as required.

GARLIC PASTE

6 large garlic bulbs

vegetable oil, as needed

1 Peel the garlic cloves—the easiest way to do this is to crush them lightly with the flat of the blade of a large knife—and discard the skins.

2 Put the garlic cloves into a blender or food processor and process to a puree, adding enough vegetable oil to enable the blades to move. Transfer to an airtight container and store in the refrigerator for 6–8 weeks or freeze in small quantities and defrost as required.

GREEN CHILI PASTE

handful of fresh green chiles

vegetable oil, as needed

1 Wash and pat dry the green chiles. Trim off the stems and coarsely chop the flesh, leaving in the seeds, if desired.

2 Transfer to a blender or food processor and process to a puree, adding enough vegetable oil to enable the blades to move. Transfer to an airtight container and store in the refrigerator for 6–8 weeks or freeze in small quantities and defrost as required.

GHEE

2 sticks butter

1 Melt the butter in a large, heavy saucepan over medium heat and continue simmering until a thick foam appears on the surface of the butter.

2 Simmer, uncovered, for 15–20 minutes, or until the foam separates, the milk solids settle on the bottom, and the liquid becomes clear and golden. Watch closely, because the milk solids at the bottom of the pan can burn quickly.

3 Meanwhile, line a strainer with a piece of cheesecloth and place the strainer over a bowl. Slowly pour the liquid through the cloth, without disturbing the milk solids at the bottom of the pan. Discard the milk solids.

4 Let the ghee cool, then transfer to a smaller container, cover, and chill. Store in the refrigerator for up to 4 weeks.

GARAM MASALA

2 bay leaves, crumbled

2 cinnamon sticks, broken in half

seeds from 8 green cardamom pods

2 tablespoons cumin seeds

1½ tablespoons coriander seeds

1½ tablespoons black peppercorns

1 teaspoon cloves

¼ teaspoon ground cloves

1 Heat a dry skillet over high heat until a splash of water "dances" when it hits the surface. Reduce the heat to medium, add the bay leaves, cinnamon sticks, cardamom seeds, cumin seeds, coriander seeds, peppercorns, and whole cloves, and dry-fry, stirring constantly, until the cumin seeds look dark golden brown and you can smell the aromas. Immediately remove the spices from the pan and let cool.

2 Use a spice grinder or mortar and pestle to grind the spices to a fine powder. Stir in the ground cloves. Store in an airtight container for up to 2 months.

PANEER

9¼ cups milk

⅓ cup lemon juice

1 Pour the milk into a large, heavy saucepan over high heat and bring to a boil. Remove the pan from the heat and stir in the lemon juice. Return the pan to the heat and continue boiling for an additional minute, until the curds and whey separate and the liquid is clear.

2 Remove the pan from the heat and set aside for an hour or so until the milk is completely cool. Meanwhile, line a strainer with a piece of cheesecloth large enough to hang over the edge and place the strainer over a bowl.

3 Pour the cold curds and whey into the cloth, then gather up the edges and squeeze out all the excess moisture.

4 Use a piece of string to tightly tie the cheesecloth around the curds in a ball. Put the ball into a bowl and place a plate on top. Place a can of beans or soup on the plate to weigh down the curds, then chill for at least 12 hours. The curds will press into a compact mass that can be cut. Store in the refrigerator for up to 3 days.

PAO BHAJI MASALA

2 tablespoons coriander seeds

1 tablespoon cumin seeds

1 teaspoon fennel seeds

1 star anise

4 dried red chiles

6 cloves

¼ teaspoon cardamom seeds

1 cinnamon stick

1 teaspoon ground turmeric

1 tablespoon dried mango powder

1 tablespoon garam masala

1 teaspoon ground ginger

1 Heat a nonstick skillet over medium heat. Gently roast the coriander seeds, cumin seeds, fennel seeds, star anise, dried red chiles, cloves, cardamom seeds, and cinnamon stick until they turn slightly darker and begin to release their aroma. Remove from the heat and let cool.

2 Use a spice grinder or mortar and pestle to grind all the whole spices to a fine powder. Stir in the remaining ingredients. Store in an airtight container for up to 2 months.

TANDOORI MASALA

2 teaspoons garlic powder

2 teaspoons ground ginger

1 teaspoon ground cloves

1 teaspoon ground cardamom seeds

1 teaspoon ground fenugreek

1 teaspoon ground cinnamon

1 teaspoon pepper

¼ teaspoon ground nutmeg

1 tablespoon ground cumin

1 tablespoon cayenne pepper or chili powder

2 tablespoons ground coriander

1 Put all the ingredients into a bowl and stir to mix well. Store in an airtight container for up to 2 months.

SAMBHAR MASALA

3 dried red chiles, stems removed

2 tablespoons coriander seeds

2 teaspoons cumin seeds

2 teaspoons black mustard seeds

1 teaspoon black peppercorns

1 teaspoon fenugreek seeds

3 cloves

¼ teaspoon ground turmeric

½ teaspoon asafetida or garlic powder

1½ teaspoon vegetable oil or peanut oil

1½ tablespoons split yellow lentils (chana dal)

1 tablespoon dry unsweetened coconut

1½ tablespoons split black lentils (urad dal chilke)

1 Heat a large, heavy saucepan over medium–high heat. Add the dried red chiles, coriander seeds, cumin seeds, black mustard seeds, peppercorns, fenugreek seeds, and cloves and dry-fry, stirring constantly, until the mustard seeds start to pop, you can smell the aromas, and the seeds darken but do not burn. Stir in the turmeric and asafetida, then immediately transfer the spices to a bowl.

2 Return the pan to the heat. Add the oil and heat, then stir in the split yellow lentils, coconut, and split black lentils and cook for about 1 minute, until they darken. Transfer to the bowl of spices. Let the mixture cool completely.

3 Use a spice grinder or mortar and pestle to grind to a fine powder. Store in an airtight container for up to 2 months.

CHAPTER 1
RAITAS, CHUTNEYS & PICKLES

Kheera ka raita

CUCUMBER RAITA

This is the all-purpose, everyday accompaniment that is served with almost any spicy Indian dish. The creaminess of the yogurt and the coolness of the cucumber help to temper the heat of fiery dishes.

SERVES: 4

PREP: 15 minutes

COOK: 1–2 minutes, plus cooling time

1 small cucumber

¾ cup plain yogurt

¼ teaspoon sugar

¼ teaspoon salt

1 teaspoon cumin seeds

10–12 black peppercorns

¼ teaspoon paprika

1 Peel the cucumber and scoop out the seeds. Cut the flesh into bite-size pieces and set aside.

2 Put the yogurt into a bowl and beat with a fork until smooth. Add the sugar and salt and mix well.

3 Preheat a small, heavy saucepan over medium–high heat. When the pan is hot, turn off the heat and add the cumin seeds and peppercorns. Stir around for 40–50 seconds, until they release their aroma. Remove from the pan and let cool for 5 minutes, then crush in a mortar with a pestle.

4 Reserve ¼ teaspoon of this mixture and stir the remainder into the yogurt. Add the cucumber and stir to mix.

5 Transfer the raita to a serving dish and sprinkle with the reserved toasted spices and the paprika.

TIP

For a flavor variation, try adding a little lemon zest and juice, or stirring in some chopped fresh mint just before serving.

Aam aur annanas raita

MANGO & PINEAPPLE RAITA

Yogurt, or "curd," as it is known in India, is a staple throughout the regions. It is eaten plain or in raitas with vegetables and fruit added. This cooling yogurt salad includes juicy diced pineapple and mango.

SERVES: 4

PREP: 10–15 minutes

COOK: 1–2 minutes

1 cup plain yogurt

1 onion, finely sliced

1 tomato, finely chopped

1 fresh green chile, finely chopped

⅔ cup finely diced pineapple flesh

⅔ cup finely diced ripe mango

¼ teaspoon salt

2 tablespoons vegetable oil or peanut oil

1 teaspoon black mustard seeds

4 fresh curry leaves

1 Put the yogurt into a bowl and whisk until smooth.

2 Add the onion, tomato, chile, pineapple, mango, and salt to the yogurt and stir to mix well.

3 Heat the oil in a small skillet, then add the mustard seeds and curry leaves. Cook, stirring constantly, for a few seconds until the mustard seeds start to pop.

4 Remove the pan from the heat and pour the contents over the yogurt mixture. Stir gently to mix and serve immediately or chill until required.

TIP

This raita can be stored, covered, in the refrigerator and used within 2 days.

Anaar ka raita

SOUTH INDIAN YOGURT, POMEGRANATE & PEANUT RAITA

Also known as a *pachadi* in southern India, this cooling accompaniment is made more often than not with yogurt, sautéed spices, and freshly grated coconut. A pachadi accompanies the main meal and is one of the dishes that makes up the *sadya* or south Indian vegetarian platter.

SERVES: 4

PREP: 10 minutes

COOK: 4–5 minutes

2 tablespoons vegetable oil or peanut oil

4 shallots, finely chopped

2 fresh green chiles, finely chopped

2 teaspoons finely grated fresh ginger

1 teaspoon black mustard seeds

4 fresh curry leaves

2 whole dried red chiles, broken in half

2 teaspoons cumin seeds

1 cup plain yogurt, whisked

1 teaspoon salt

¼ cup freshly grated coconut

2 tablespoons finely chopped fresh cilantro

2 tablespoons pomegranate seeds

2 tablespoons coarsely chopped toasted peanuts

1 Heat the oil in a skillet, add the shallots, and sauté over low heat for 3–4 minutes.

2 Add the green chiles, ginger, mustard seeds, curry leaves, dried red chiles, and cumin seeds. Sauté for 1 minute, then remove from the heat.

3 Stir in the yogurt, salt, coconut, and cilantro. Stir to mix well and transfer to a serving bowl. Sprinkle with the pomegranate seeds and peanuts just before serving.

Bhindi ka raita

CRISPY OKRA RAITA

This delightful raita, from the western shores of India, is thick and cooling on the palate when served with a hot curry or spicy fried fish and rice. The crisp okra provides texture to this slightly sweet and gently spiced dish.

SERVES: 4   **PREP:** 10 minutes   **COOK:** 5–6 minutes

⅓ cup plus 1 tablespoon vegetable oil or peanut oil

8 ounces okra, trimmed and cut into ½-inch slices

1¾ cups plain yogurt

1 teaspoon salt

1 teaspoon sugar

1 teaspoon cayenne pepper

¼ teaspoon ground turmeric

1 teaspoon black mustard seeds

2 tablespoons finely chopped fresh cilantro

1 Heat ⅓ cup of the oil in a large skillet over medium heat. When the oil is hot, add the okra, toss, and cook, stirring occasionally, for 3–4 minutes; the okra will slowly turn crisp and brown. Once the okra is well browned, transfer to paper towels and set aside until ready to serve.

2 Whisk the yogurt with the salt and sugar in a medium serving bowl. Sprinkle the cayenne pepper and turmeric over the yogurt mixture, but do not mix it in.

3 Heat the remaining oil in a small skillet over high heat. When the oil begins to smoke, add the mustard seeds. When the mustard seeds stop popping, pour the hot oil directly on top of the cayenne pepper and turmeric. (This will cook the spices without burning them.)

4 Just before serving, place the crisp okra on top and sprinkle with the chopped cilantro.

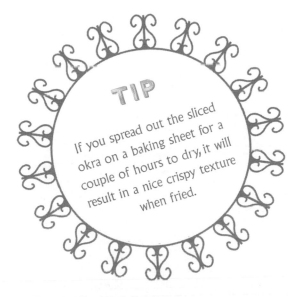

TIP

If you spread out the sliced okra on a baking sheet for a couple of hours to dry, it will result in a nice crispy texture when fried.

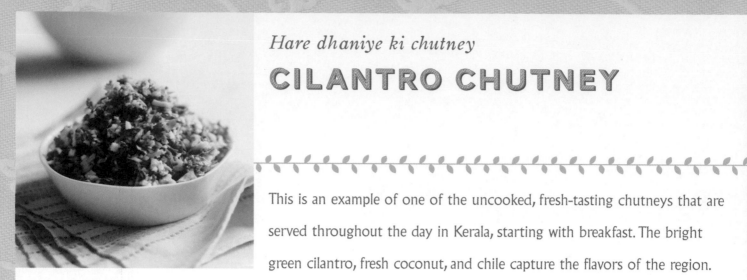

Hare dhaniye ki chutney

CILANTRO CHUTNEY

This is an example of one of the uncooked, fresh-tasting chutneys that are served throughout the day in Kerala, starting with breakfast. The bright green cilantro, fresh coconut, and chile capture the flavors of the region.

SERVES: 4

PREP: 5–10 minutes

COOK: 0 minutes

1½ tablespoons lemon juice

1½ tablespoons cold water

2 cups coarsely chopped fresh cilantro leaves and stems

2 tablespoons chopped fresh coconut

1 small shallot, minced

¼-inch piece fresh ginger, chopped

1 fresh green chile, seeded and chopped

½ teaspoon sugar, or to taste

½ teaspoon salt, or to taste

pinch of pepper, or to taste

1 Put the lemon juice and water into a small food processor, add half the cilantro, and process until it is blended and a slushy paste forms. Gradually add the remaining cilantro and process until it is all blended, scraping down the sides of the processor, if necessary. If you don't have a processor that will cope with this small quantity, use a mortar and pestle, adding the cilantro in small amounts.

2 Add the remaining ingredients and continue processing until they are all finely chopped and blended. Taste and adjust the seasoning, adding extra sugar and salt, if needed. Transfer to a nonmetallic bowl and serve immediately or cover and chill until required.

TIP

For a cooling cilantro raita, stir 1¼ cups plain yogurt into the chutney and chill for at least 1 hour.

Mirch aur pyaaz ki chutney
CHILE & ONION CHUTNEY

For those who like really hot and spicy food, this fresh chutney packs a punch. Gujarati people will include the chile seeds and serve this at all meals, eating it in the summer as a snack with poppadoms or pooris.

SERVES: 4

PREP: 5–10 minutes, plus standing & chilling time

COOK: 0 minutes

1–2 fresh green chiles, finely chopped (seeded, if desired)

1 small fresh Thai chile, finely chopped (seeded, if desired)

1 tablespoon white wine vinegar or apple cider vinegar

2 onions, finely chopped

2 tablespoons lemon juice

1 tablespoon sugar

3 tablespoons chopped fresh cilantro, mint, or parsley, or a combination of herbs

salt, to taste

chile flower, to garnish (see TIP)

1 Put the chiles into a small, nonmetallic bowl with the vinegar, stir around, and then drain. Return the chiles to the bowl and stir in the onions, lemon juice, sugar, and herbs, then add salt.

2 Let stand at room temperature or cover and chill for 15 minutes. Garnish with the chile flower before serving.

TIP

To make a chile flower, make several lengthwise cuts along the chile, keeping the stem intact. Place the chile in a bowl of ice water for 25–30 minutes.

Imli ki chutney

TAMARIND CHUTNEY

There isn't any mistaking the fresh, sour taste of tamarind—it adds a distinctive flavor to many dishes, especially those from southern India. More like a sauce than a thick chutney, this sweet-and-sour mixture is essential for serving with samosas.

SERVES: 4–6

PREP: 5–10 minutes

COOK: 35–40 minutes, plus cooling time

1 cup chopped tamarind pulp

2 cups cold water

½ fresh Thai chile, or to taste, seeded and chopped

¼ cup firmly packed light brown sugar, or to taste

½ teaspoon salt, or to taste

1 Put the tamarind and water into a heavy saucepan over high heat and bring to a boil. Reduce the heat to the lowest setting and simmer, stirring occasionally to break up the tamarind pulp, for 25 minutes, or until tender.

2 Transfer the tamarind pulp to a strainer and use a wooden spoon to push the pulp into a clean pan.

3 Stir in the chile, sugar, and salt and continue simmering for an additional 10 minutes, or until the desired consistency is reached. Let cool slightly, then taste and stir in extra sugar or salt, if needed.

4 Let cool completely, then serve immediately or chill until required.

Aam ki chutney

MANGO CHUTNEY

This fresh-tasting, spiced chutney is about as far as one can get from the thick, gloopy, and overly sweet mango chutney that can be bought prepared in jars. With its punchy flavors and zingy color, it will bring a touch of Goan sunshine to any Indian meal.

SERVES: 4–6

PREP: 10 minutes, plus chilling time

COOK: 20 minutes

1 large mango (about 1 pound), peeled, pitted, and finely chopped

2 tablespoons lime juice

1 tablespoon vegetable oil or peanut oil

2 shallots, finely chopped

1 garlic clove, finely chopped

2 fresh green chiles, seeded and finely sliced

1 teaspoon black mustard seeds

1 teaspoon coriander seeds

⅓ cup palm sugar or firmly packed light brown sugar

⅓ cup white wine vinegar

1 teaspoon salt

pinch of ground ginger

1 Put the mango into a nonmetallic bowl with the lime juice and set aside.

2 Heat the oil in a large skillet or saucepan over medium–high heat. Add the shallots and cook for about 3 minutes. Add the garlic and chiles and stir for an additional 2 minutes, or until the shallots are soft but not brown. Add the mustard seeds and coriander seeds and then stir.

3 Add the mango to the pan with the palm sugar, vinegar, salt, and ground ginger and stir. Reduce the heat to its lowest setting and simmer for 10 minutes, until the liquid thickens and the mango becomes sticky.

4 Remove from the heat and let cool completely. Transfer to an airtight container, cover, and chill for about 3 days before using.

TIP

The chutney should be stored in the refrigerator. Once opened, it should be used within a week.

Nariyal sambal

COCONUT SAMBAL

Coconuts grow in abundance along the gently flowing backwaters of Kerala, and slightly crunchy fresh chutneys such as this are popular. Serve as a snack with poppadoms or as an accompaniment to simply cooked seafood.

SERVES: 2–4

PREP: 5–10 minutes

COOK: 0 minutes

½ fresh coconut or 1¾ cups dry unsweetened coconut

2 fresh green chiles, chopped (seeded, if desired)

1-inch piece fresh ginger, finely chopped

¼ cup chopped fresh cilantro

2 tablespoons lemon juice, or to taste

2 shallots, minced

1 If you are using a whole coconut, use a hammer and nail to punch a hole into the "eye" of the coconut, then pour out the water from the inside and reserve. Use the hammer to break the coconut in half, then peel and chop one half.

2 Put the chopped coconut and the chiles into a food processor and process for about 30 seconds, until finely chopped. Add the ginger, cilantro, and lemon juice and process again.

3 If the mixture seems too dry, stir in about 1 tablespoon of coconut water or water. Stir in the shallots and serve immediately, or cover and chill until required.

TIP

The sambal will keep its fresh flavor for up to 3 days if stored in the refrigerator.

Cuchumber

TOMATO KACHUMBAR

This popular tomato-and-cucumber salad is easy to make and its vibrant colors are pleasing to the eye. It makes a refreshing accompaniment to a variety of dishes, such as grilled or broiled skewered meats.

SERVES: 6

PREP: 10–15 minutes, plus chilling time

COOK: 0 minutes

½ cup lime juice

½ teaspoon sugar

pinch of salt

6 tomatoes, chopped

½ cucumber, chopped

8 scallions, chopped

1 fresh green chile, seeded and chopped

1 tablespoon chopped fresh cilantro

1 tablespoon chopped fresh mint

1. Mix together the lime juice, sugar, and salt in a large bowl and stir until the sugar has completely dissolved.

2. Add the tomatoes, cucumber, scallions, chile, cilantro, and mint and toss well to mix.

3. Cover and chill in the refrigerator for at least 30 minutes. Toss the salad before serving.

TIP

This salad is best eaten on the day of making, before it turns soggy. If desired, lemon juice can be used instead of lime juice.

Nimbu ka aachar

LIME PICKLE

With chunky pieces of lime and mouthwatering spices, this tangy pickle is an ideal accompaniment to a variety of dishes. It's easy to make but requires time and patience—you'll need to start preparing it a month in advance if you plan to serve it on a particular occasion.

SERVES: 4–6

PREP: 10 minutes, plus marinating time

COOK: 5 minutes

12 limes, halved and seeded

⅓ cup salt

⅔ cup chili powder

¼ cup dry mustard

¼ cup ground fenugreek

1 tablespoon ground turmeric

1¼ cups chili oil

1½ tablespoons yellow mustard seeds, crushed

½ teaspoon asafetida

1 Cut each lime half into wedges and pack them into a large sterilized jar, sprinkling with the salt at the same time. Cover and let stand in a warm place for 10–14 days, or until the limes have turned brown and softened.

2 Mix together the chili powder, mustard powder, fenugreek, and turmeric in a small bowl and add to the jar of limes. Stir to mix, then replace the cover and let stand for 2 days.

3 Transfer the lime mixture to a heatproof bowl. Heat the oil in a heavy skillet. Add the mustard seeds and asafetida to the pan and cook, stirring constantly, until the oil is hot and just beginning to smoke.

4 Pour the oil and spices over the limes and mix well. Cover and let cool. When cool, pack into a sterilized jar, seal, and store in a warm place (preferably on a sunny kitchen windowsill) for 1 week before serving.

Hari mirchi aachar

GREEN CHILE PICKLE

This chile pickle is a great way to spice up any meal. Indian meals are generally served with different condiments, of which pickles are the most common. This is a classic hot and spicy pickle—not for the fainthearted by any means.

SERVES: 4–6

PREP: 30 minutes

COOK: 2–3 minutes

20 fresh green chiles

3 tablespoons ground coriander

1–1½ tablespoons fennel seeds

1 teaspoon fenugreek seeds

1 teaspoon black mustard seeds

pinch of asafetida

1 tablespoon salt

1 teaspoon dried mango powder (amchoor)

½ teaspoon ground turmeric

¼ cup peanut oil combined with 2 teaspoons dry mustard

2 tablespoons white wine vinegar

1 Wash and dry the chiles and cut a slit lengthwise in each.

2 Put the ground coriander, fennel seeds, fenugreek seeds, and mustard seeds into a spice grinder and grind coarsely. Transfer to a bowl.

3 Add the asafetida, salt, dried mango powder, and turmeric to the bowl and mix well.

4 Heat the oil and dry mustard in a skillet until hot, then stir in the spice mixture. Cook, stirring constantly, for 1 minute and remove from the heat. Add the vinegar and stir to mix well.

5 Stuff the chiles with the spice mix and pack into a large sterilized jar. Seal and store in a warm place (preferably on a sunny kitchen windowsill) for up to 2 days before using. This pickle can be refrigerated for up to a month.

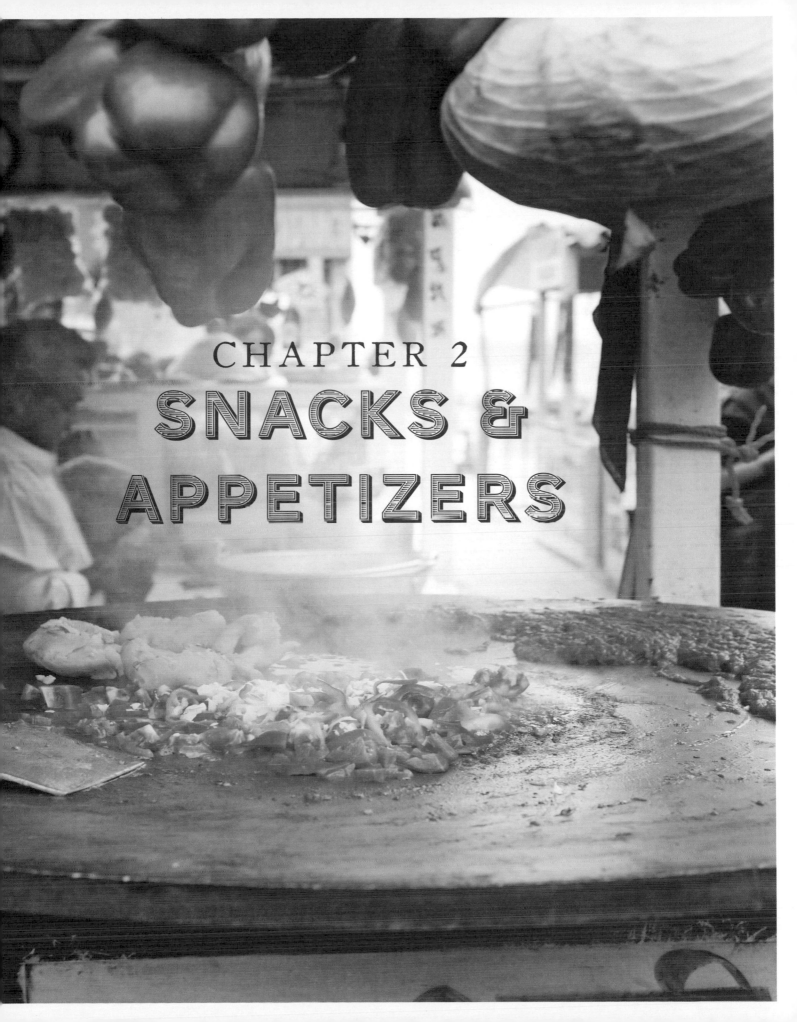

CHAPTER 2
SNACKS & APPETIZERS

Aloo mattar samosa

VEGETARIAN SAMOSAS

It takes a little practice and patience to master the art of shaping these triangular pastries, but after you've rolled out and filled a couple, you will quickly get the hang of it. For a meat-based filling, try using *keema mattar* (see page 140), making sure to simmer the mixture until it is dry before using.

MAKES: 14

PREP: 40–45 minutes, plus resting time

COOK: 1 hour

2 cups all-purpose flour

½ teaspoon salt

3 tablespoons ghee or butter, melted, plus extra for greasing

1½ teaspoons lemon juice

⅓–½ cup cold water

vegetable oil or peanut oil, for deep-frying

FILLING

¼ cup ghee or vegetable oil or peanut oil

1 onion, finely chopped

2 garlic cloves, crushed

1 potato, finely diced

2 carrots, finely chopped

2 teaspoons mild, medium, or hot curry powder, to taste

1½ teaspoons ground coriander

1 teaspoon ground turmeric

1 fresh green chile, seeded and finely chopped

1 teaspoon salt

½ teaspoon black mustard seeds

1¼ cups cold water

⅔ cup frozen peas

⅓ cup finely chopped cauliflower florets

1 To make the filling, melt the ghee in a large skillet over medium–high heat. Add the onion and garlic and sauté for 5–8 minutes, until soft but not brown. Stir in the potato and carrots and continue cooking, stirring occasionally, for 5 minutes. Stir in the curry powder, ground coriander, turmeric, chile, salt, and mustard seeds. Pour in the water and bring to a boil. Reduce the heat to low and simmer, uncovered, for about 15 minutes, stirring occasionally. Add the peas and cauliflower and continue simmering until all the vegetables are tender and the liquid has evaporated. Remove from the heat and set aside.

2 Meanwhile, sift the flour and salt into a bowl. Make a well in the center, add the ghee and lemon juice, and work them into the flour with your fingertips. Gradually add the water until the mixture comes together to form a soft dough. Transfer the dough to a work surface and knead for about 10 minutes, until smooth. Shape into a ball, cover with a damp dish towel, and let rest for about 15 minutes.

3 Divide the dough into seven equal pieces. Work with one piece at a time and keep the remaining pieces covered with a dish towel. On a lightly greased work surface, roll each piece of dough into an 8-inch circle, then cut in half to make two semicircles.

4 Working with one semicircle at a time, wet the edges with water. Place about 2 teaspoons of the filling on the dough, just off-center. Fold one side into the center, covering the filling. Fold the other side in the opposite direction, overlapping the first fold to form a cone shape. Wet the open edge with more water and press down to seal.

5 Heat enough oil for deep-frying in a large saucepan or deep fryer until it reaches 350–375°F, or until a cube of bread browns in 30 seconds. Working in batches, deep-fry the samosas for 2–3 minutes, flipping them over once, until golden brown. Remove with a slotted spoon and drain well on paper towels. Serve warm or at room temperature.

Kele ke chips

PLANTAIN CHIPS

These plaintain chips are very addictive, so cook plenty. They are delicious served straight from the pan. In Kerala, unripe green bananas are cooked in the same way in coconut oil and sprinkled with salt before serving.

SERVES: 4

PREP: 10 minutes

COOK: 10–12 minutes

4 ripe plantains

1 teaspoon mild, medium, or hot curry powder, to taste

vegetable oil or peanut oil, for deep-frying

chutney, to serve

1 Peel the plantains, then cut widthwise into ⅛-inch slices. Put the slices in a bowl, sprinkle with the curry powder, and use your hands to toss lightly.

2 Heat enough oil for deep-frying in a large saucepan or deep fryer to 350–375°F, or until a cube of bread browns in 30 seconds. Deep-fry the plaintain slices, in batches, for 2 minutes, or until golden.

3 Remove the plantain chips from the pan with a slotted spoon and drain well on paper towels. Serve hot with chutney.

TIP

Ordinary yellow-skinned bananas can also be used in this recipe, but the flavor will be sweeter and they will take a little less time to cook.

Batata vadas

DEEP-FRIED POTATO BALLS

These delightful potato balls are eaten all over India as a snack or part of a main meal. Diced, boiled potatoes are combined with various flavorings, then rolled into balls, battered, and deep-fried.

SERVES: 4

PREP: 15–20 minutes

COOK: 15–20 minutes

4 russet or Yukon gold potatoes (about 1 pound), boiled and diced

1 onion, chopped

1-inch piece fresh ginger, finely chopped

1 fresh green chile, seeded and finely chopped

1 tablespoon chopped fresh cilantro

1 tablespoon lemon juice

2 teaspoons dried mango powder (amchoor)

vegetable oil or peanut oil, for deep-frying

salt, to taste

chutney, to serve

BATTER

1¼ cups chickpea (besan) flour

¼ teaspoon baking powder

¼ teaspoon chili powder

pinch of salt

about ⅔ cup cold water

1. To make the batter, sift the flour, baking powder, chili powder, and salt into a bowl. Gradually stir in enough of the water to make a smooth batter. Cover with plastic wrap and set aside.

2. Put the potatoes, onion, ginger, chile, cilantro, lemon juice, and dried mango powder into a separate bowl. Mix well with a wooden spoon, breaking up the potatoes. Season with salt. Break off small pieces of the mixture and form into balls between the palms of your hands.

3. Heat enough oil for deep-frying in a large saucepan or deep fryer to 350–375°F, or until a cube of bread browns in 30 seconds. Working in batches, dip the potato balls in the batter, using a fork, and add to the hot oil. Deep-fry for 3–4 minutes, until golden brown. Remove with a slotted spoon and drain on paper towels. Serve hot with chutney.

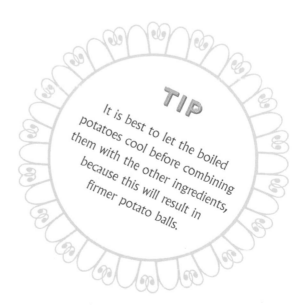

TIP

It is best to let the boiled potatoes cool before combining them with the other ingredients, because this will result in firmer potato balls.

Mirchi pakora

STUFFED CHILE BHAJIS

Also called _mirapakaya bajjilu_ or _bajji_ in Telagu, this snack of chiles stuffed with a spiced potato mixture is a specialty from Andhra Pradesh in central India and is classic street food. Serve it with your favorite chutney or a little plain yogurt.

MAKES: 8

PREP: 20 minutes, plus soaking time

COOK: 10 minutes

8 large, mild fresh green chiles

vegetable oil or peanut oil, for deep-frying

BATTER

2¾ cups chickpea (besan) flour

¾ cup rice flour

½ teaspoon baking powder

1 teaspoon ground cumin

2 teaspoons salt

1 teaspoon chili powder

about 3 cups cold water

STUFFING

2 tablespoons vegetable oil or peanut oil

1 teaspoon fennel seeds

2 teaspoon black mustard seeds

1 teaspoon cumin seeds

1 russet or Yukon gold potato, peeled, boiled, and mashed

3 tablespoons finely chopped fresh cilantro

1 teaspoon salt

½ teaspoon tamarind paste

1 tablespoon roasted peanuts, coarsely chopped

1 Slit the chiles lengthwise and remove all the seeds, using a small teaspoon. Soak the chiles in boiling water for 5 minutes. Drain on paper towels and set aside.

2 Mix together the batter ingredients with enough of the water to make a thin batter with the consistency of heavy cream. Set aside.

3 For the stuffing, heat the oil in a saucepan. Add the fennel seeds, mustard seeds, and cumin seeds. When the seeds start to pop, add the potato, cilantro, and salt and mix well. Add the tamarind paste and sprinkle with the roasted peanuts. Remove from the heat and mash until evenly combined.

4 Using your fingers, stuff the green chiles with the potato mixture.

5 Heat enough oil for deep-frying in a large saucepan or deep fryer to 350–375°F, or until a cube of bread browns in 30 seconds. Working in batches, dip the stuffed green chiles in the batter and deep-fry for 2–3 minutes, or until crisp and golden. Remove with a slotted spoon and drain on paper towels. Serve warm.

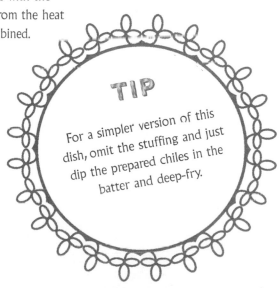

TIP

For a simpler version of this dish, omit the stuffing and just dip the prepared chiles in the batter and deep-fry.

रवान म

KHAN M

←

गिफ्ट

ARKET

Khandvi

SPICED CHICKPEA FLOUR ROLLS

Making these delicate and delicious lightly spiced chickpea flour rolls from Gujarat is almost like making an Indian-style pasta. There is an art to making and rolling the *khandvi,* and it may take more than a few attempts to get perfect-looking ones, although the taste will be great every time.

MAKES: 24

PREP: 15–20 minutes

COOK: 20 minutes, plus standing time

vegetable oil or peanut oil, for greasing

2¾ cups chickpea (besan) flour, sifted

½ cup plain yogurt

2½ cups warm water

2 teaspoons salt

¼ teaspoon ground turmeric

2 teaspoons grated fresh ginger

2 garlic cloves, crushed

4 teaspoons green chili paste (see page 26)

TOPPING

⅓ cup vegetable oil or peanut oil

1 teaspoon sesame seeds

1 teaspoon black mustard seeds

¼ cup finely chopped fresh cilantro

2 tablespoons freshly grated coconut

1 Lightly brush four large baking sheets with oil and set aside.

2 Put the chickpea flour, yogurt, and water into a heavy saucepan with the salt, turmeric, ginger, garlic, and green chili paste. Whisk until smooth, then place over medium heat and continue to whisk constantly. When the batter starts to thicken after 5–6 minutes, reduce the heat to low, cover, and cook for 4–5 minutes. Stir, replace the cover, and cook for an additional 2–3 minutes, or until thickened and smooth.

3 Remove from the heat and ladle the batter onto the prepared baking sheets, using a spatula to spread the mixture as thinly as possible. The batter will start to set as it cools. Let stand for 5 minutes, then slice it lengthwise into 2-inch-wide strips. This quantity should make about 24 rolls.

4 Starting at one end of each strip, use the spatula to gently lift and roll (like a small jelly roll). Repeat until all the strips have been rolled. Transfer to a serving plate.

5 Meanwhile, make the topping. Heat the oil in a skillet and add the sesame seeds and mustard seeds. When they start to pop, remove from the heat and drizzle this spiced oil over the chickpea flour rolls. Sprinkle with the cilantro and coconut. Serve warm or at room temperature.

Sabudana aloo wada

TAPIOCA & POTATO CAKES

These potato and tapioca cakes from western and southern India are usually served as a snack with _masala chai_ (tea). Tapioca pearls are made from a starch extracted from the cassava root. They come in various sizes and can be found in any Asian grocery store.

MAKES: 15–20

PREP: 10–15 minutes, plus soaking time

COOK: 25–30 minutes

2 potatoes, peeled and coarsely chopped

1⅓ cups medium tapioca pearls

1 cup cold water

2 fresh red chiles, finely chopped

1 teaspoon cumin seeds

1 teaspoon salt

¼ cup finely chopped fresh cilantro

vegetable oil or peanut oil, for deep-frying

1 Put the potatoes into a saucepan of boiling water. Boil for 12–15 minutes, or until just tender. Drain thoroughly and transfer to a mixing bowl.

2 Meanwhile, put the tapioca into a bowl and pour the water over it. Let soak for 12–15 minutes, or until the water has been absorbed and the tapioca is swollen. Transfer to a strainer to drain away any excess liquid.

3 Add the chiles, cumin seeds, salt, and cilantro to the potatoes and mash until fairly smooth. Stir in the soaked tapioca and stir to mix well. With wet hands, roll the mixture into 15–20 walnut-size balls, then flatten to make patties.

4 Heat enough oil for deep-frying in a large saucepan or deep fryer to 350–375°F, or until a cube of bread browns in 30 seconds. Working in batches, deep-fry the tapioca and potato cakes for 3–4 minutes, or until golden brown. Remove with a slotted spoon and drain on paper towels. Serve warm.

TIP

The mixture for these delicious potato cakes can be made up to a day in advance, formed into patties and stored, covered, in the refrigerator until ready to cook.

Paneer tikka

PANEER TIKKA

For India's millions of vegetarians, *paneer* (a firm, white cheese) is the main source of dietary protein. It has little taste on its own, which is why it is paired here with a hot, spicy tikka paste.

MAKES: 4

PREP: 15–20 minutes, plus marinating time

COOK: 15–20 minutes

12 ounce paneer, halloumi cheese, or tofu, cut into 16 cubes

vegetable oil or peanut oil, for brushing

1 teaspoon garam masala

fresh cilantro leaves, to garnish

TIKKA PASTE

10 black peppercorns

6 cloves

seeds from 4 green cardamom pods

1 teaspoon cumin seeds

1 teaspoon coriander seeds

½ teaspoon poppy seeds

½ teaspoon chili powder

½ teaspoon ground turmeric

1 tablespoon garlic paste

1 tablespoon ginger paste

½ small onion, chopped

⅔ cup plain yogurt

1½ teaspoons tomato paste

1 tablespoon chickpea (besan) flour

1 tablespoon vegetable oil or peanut oil

1 To make the tikka paste, dry-fry the peppercorns, cloves, cardamom seeds, cumin seeds, coriander seeds, and poppy seeds in a skillet over high heat, stirring constantly, until you can smell the aroma. Immediately remove the spices from the pan, so they don't burn.

2 Put the spices into a spice grinder or use a mortar and pestle. Add the chili powder and turmeric and grind to a fine powder. Add the garlic paste, ginger paste, and onion and continue grinding until a paste forms. Transfer to a large bowl and stir in the yogurt, tomato paste, chickpea flour, and oil.

3 Add the paneer to the bowl and use your hands to coat the cubes in the tikka paste, being careful not to break up the pieces of cheese. Let marinate at room temperature for 30 minutes, or cover the bowl with plastic wrap and chill for up to 24 hours.

4 Preheat the broiler to medium–high. If you have refrigerated the cheese, remove it from the refrigerator 15 minutes before cooking. Lightly brush four metal skewers with oil. Drain the paneer and thread it onto the skewers, leaving a little space between each cube.

5 Cook the skewers under the preheated broiler for 12–15 minutes, turning them over once and basting with any remaining tikka paste, until the paneer is lightly charred on the edges.

6 To serve, sprinkle the hot kabobs with the garam masala and garnish with cilantro leaves.

Gobhi ka pakora

GOLDEN CAULIFLOWER FRITTERS

These golden fritters are made from cauliflower florets dipped into a spiced batter and deep-fried until crisp. They are delicious as a snack, served with chutney for dipping, or as part of a meal.

SERVES: 4

PREP: 10–15 minutes, plus standing time

COOK: 20–25 minutes

vegetable oil or peanut oil, for deep-frying

3 cups cauliflower florets

chutney, to serve

BATTER

1½ cups chickpea (besan) flour

2 teaspoons ground coriander

1 teaspoon garam masala

1 teaspoon salt

½ teaspoon ground turmeric

pinch of chili powder

1 tablespoon ghee, melted, or vegetable oil or peanut oil

1 teaspoon lemon juice

⅔ cup cold water

2 teaspoons nigella seeds

1 To make the batter, stir the chickpea flour, ground coriander, garam masala, salt, turmeric, and chili powder into a large bowl. Make a well in the center, add the ghee and lemon juice with 2 tablespoons of the water, and stir to make a thick batter. Slowly beat in enough of the remaining water with an electric handheld mixer or a whisk to make a smooth batter with the consistency of heavy cream. Stir in the nigella seeds. Cover the bowl with plastic wrap and set aside for at least 30 minutes.

2 Heat enough oil for deep-frying in a large saucepan or deep fryer to 350–375°F, or until a cube of bread browns in 30 seconds. Dip one cauliflower floret at a time into the batter and let any excess batter drip back into the bowl, then drop the cauliflower floret into the hot oil. Add a few more batter-dipped cauliflower florets, without overcrowding the pan, and fry for about 3 minutes, or until golden brown and crisp.

3 Use a slotted spoon to remove the fritters from the oil and drain well on paper towels. Continue frying until all the cauliflower florets and batter have been used. Serve the fritters with chutney for dipping.

Pyaaz pakora

SPICY ONION FRITTERS

These seriously tasty spicy onion fritters are extremely difficult to resist. They are a popular snack all over India and can often be found among the foods offered from the roadside stalls or carts of the numerous street vendors. They are best enjoyed with chutney for dipping.

SERVES: 4

PREP: 10–15 minutes

COOK: 25–30 minutes

1⅔ cups chickpea (besan) flour

1 teaspoon salt, or to taste

small pinch of baking soda

2½ tablespoons rice flour

1 teaspoon fennel seeds

1 teaspoon cumin seeds

2 fresh green chiles, finely chopped (seeded, if preferred)

2 large onions, sliced into semicircles and separated

⅓ cup finely chopped fresh cilantro leaves and stems

about 1 cup cold water

vegetable oil or peanut oil, for deep-frying

1 Sift the besan flour into a large bowl and add the salt, baking soda, rice flour, fennel seeds, and cumin seeds. Mix together well, then add the chiles, onions, and cilantro. Gradually pour in the water and mix until a thick batter is formed and the onions are throughly coated with it.

2 Heat enough oil for deep-frying in a large saucepan or deep fryer to 350–375°F, or until a cube of bread browns in 30 seconds. Add as many small amounts (each about 1½ teaspoons) of the batter as will fit in a single layer, without overcrowding the pan. Reduce the heat slightly and cook the fritters for 8–10 minutes, until golden brown and crisp.

3 Use a slotted spoon to remove the fritters from the oil and drain well on paper towels. Continue frying until all the batter mixture has been used. Serve hot.

Kadhi

SPICED YOGURT SOUP

Kadhi is a traditional Gujarati preparation of a wonderful sweet-and-spicy yogurt mixture thickened with chickpea flour. This authentic Gujarati-style spiced yogurt soup is slightly thinner in texture than the Punjabi version of the same dish. They both have a balance of sweet, sour, and spicy flavors.

SERVES: 4

PREP: 20 minutes

COOK: 15–20 minutes

4 cups cold water

4 cups plain yogurt

3 tablespoons chickpea (gram) flour

4 fresh green chiles, slit lengthwise

1 tablespoon freshly grated ginger

1 tablespoon palm sugar or packed light brown sugar

1 teaspoon ground turmeric

1 tablespoon vegetable oil or peanut oil

1 tablespoon ghee or butter

2 dried red chiles, broken into pieces

8 fresh curry leaves

1 teaspoon cumin seeds

½ teaspoon black mustard seeds

pinch of asafetida or garlic powder

¼ cup chopped fresh cilantro

salt, to taste

1 Mix together the water, yogurt, and chickpea flour in a large saucepan until smooth. Add the green chiles, ginger, palm sugar, turmeric, and salt. Bring the mixture to a boil, then immediately reduce the heat to low and cook, stirring frequently, for 8–10 minutes.

2 Meanwhile, heat the oil and ghee in a small skillet over medium heat. Add the dried red chiles, curry leaves, cumin seeds, mustard seeds, and asafetida and cook, stirring constantly, for 2–3 minutes, or until the seeds start to pop.

3 Stir the spiced oil into the yogurt mixture in the saucepan. Ladle into warm bowls, sprinkle with the cilantro, and serve hot.

TIP

For a thicker version of this soup, increase the quantity of chickpea flour to ⅓ cup. Be careful not to boil the yogurt for too long or it will curdle.

Pao bhaji

SPICED POTATO & VEGETABLE SNACK

This incredibly popular street snack originated in Mumbai, but is now prevalent throughout India. It consists of a potato-and-vegetable mixture and is served with warm rolls or *pao*. *Pao bhaji masala* is a prepared spice mixture that is readily available in Asian grocery stores.

SERVES: 4

PREP: 25 minutes

COOK: 45–50 minutes

¼ cup vegetable oil or peanut oil

3½ tablespoons butter

2 garlic cloves, crushed

2 fresh green chiles, finely chopped

1 large onion, finely chopped

2 teaspoon grated fresh ginger

1 (14½-ounce) can diced tomatoes

1½ cups finely chopped cauliflower

1½ cups finely chopped green cabbage

1⅓ cups fresh shelled or frozen peas

1 large carrot, shredded

4 russet potatoes, boiled, peeled, and mashed

3 tablespoons pao bhaji masala (see page 28)

2 teaspoons salt

1 tablespoon lemon juice

¼ cup finely chopped fresh cilantro

4 white rolls, to serve

1 Heat the oil and butter in a wok or large skillet over medium heat. Sauté the garlic and chiles for 30 seconds, then stir in the onion and ginger. Sauté for 8–10 minutes, or until the onion is lightly browned.

2 Add the tomatoes and sauté for 6–8 minutes, or until thickened. Stir in the cauliflower, cabbage, peas, carrot, and potatoes. Add the pao bhaji masala. Cover and cook, stirring occasionally, for 15–20 minutes.

3 Preheat the broiler. Season the potato-and-vegetable mixture with the salt and stir in the lemon juice. Remove from the heat and sprinkle with the chopped cilantro. Slice the rolls in half and lightly toast them under the preheated broiler. Serve the potato mixture in warm bowls with the toasted rolls.

Macchi pakora

GOLDEN FISH FRITTERS

These fish fritters make the most of the abundance of fresh fish in India's coastal regions. They are coated in a lightly spiced gram flour batter and deep-fried until crisp and golden.

SERVES: 4–6

½ teaspoon salt

2 tablespoons lemon juice or white wine vinegar

1½ pounds skinless white fish fillets, such as cod, halibut, or monkfish, cut into large chunks

vegetable oil or peanut oil, for deep-frying

pepper, to taste

lemon wedges, to serve

BATTER

1½ cups chickpea (besan) flour

seeds from 4 green cardamom pods

large pinch of ground turmeric

large pinch of baking soda

finely grated zest of 1 lemon

¾ cup cold water

salt and pepper, to taste

PREP: 10–15 minutes, plus marinating time

1 Combine the salt and lemon juice in a small bowl with pepper. Rub the mixture all over the fish chunks, then transfer to a nonmetallic bowl and let marinate for 20–30 minutes.

2 Meanwhile, to make the batter, put the chickpea flour into a bowl and stir in the cardamom seeds, turmeric, baking soda, lemon zest, and salt and pepper. Make a well in the center and gradually stir in the water to make a thin batter with the consistency of light cream.

3 Gently stir the pieces of fish into the batter, being careful not to break them up.

COOK: 15–20 minutes

4 Heat enough oil for deep-frying in a large saucepan or deep fryer to 350–375°F, or until a cube of bread browns in 30 seconds. Remove the fish pieces from the batter and let the excess batter drip back into the bowl. Working in batches, drop the battered fish pieces into the hot oil and deep-fry for 2½–3 minutes, until golden brown.

5 Use a slotted spoon to remove the fried fish pieces from the oil and drain on paper towels. Continue frying until all the fish has been used. Serve hot with lemon wedges for squeezing over the fish fritters.

Mahi tikka

FISH TIKKA

You need a firm-fleshed fish for these delectable fish skewers—salmon has been used here, but monkfish would work equally well. Traditionally, these would be cooked in a *tandoor* (Indian clay oven).

MAKES: 8

pinch of saffron threads, pounded

1 tablespoon hot milk

⅓ cup Greek-style yogurt

1 tablespoon garlic paste

1 tablespoon ginger paste

1 teaspoon salt, or to taste

½ teaspoon sugar

juice of ½ lemon

½–1 teaspoon chili powder

½ teaspoon garam masala

1 teaspoon ground fennel seeds

2 teaspoons chickpea (besan) flour

1½ pounds salmon fillets, skinned and cut into 2-inch cubes

3 tablespoons vegetable oil or peanut oil, plus extra for brushing

PREP: 10–15 minutes, plus soaking & marinating time

1 Soak the pounded saffron in the hot milk for 10 minutes.

2 Put all the remaining ingredients, except the fish and oil, into a bowl and beat with a fork or a whisk until smooth. Add the saffron-and-milk mixture, stir well, and add the fish cubes. Using a metal spoon, mix gently, turning the fish around until fully coated with the marinade. Cover and let marinate in the refrigerator for 2 hours. Return to room temperature before cooking.

3 Preheat the broiler to high. Brush the broiler rack generously with oil. Brush eight metal skewers lightly with oil.

COOK: 10 minutes, plus standing time

4 Thread the fish cubes onto the prepared skewers, leaving a little space between each piece. Arrange on the prepared broiler rack and cook under the preheated broiler for 3 minutes. Brush half the oil over the kabobs and cook for an additional minute. Turn over and brush any remaining marinade over the fish. Cook for 3 minutes. Brush the remaining oil over the fish and cook for an additional 2 minutes, or until the fish is lightly charred.

5 Remove the skewers from the heat and let stand for 5 minutes before serving.

Jhinga poori

SHRIMP POORIS

In this recipe, pooris—deep-fried, whole-wheat flatbreads—are topped with a spicy shrimp-and-tomato mixture. Pooris are best served straight from the pan, so if you want to avoid last-minute deep-frying, you could use chapatis or naans instead.

MAKES: 6

PREP: 10 minutes

COOK: 15–20 minutes

2 teaspoons coriander seeds

½ teaspoon black peppercorns

1 large garlic clove, crushed

1 teaspoon ground turmeric

¼–½ teaspoon chili powder

½ teaspoon salt, or to taste

3 tablespoons ghee or vegetable oil or peanut oil

1 onion, grated

1 (28-ounce) can crushed tomatoes

pinch of sugar

1 pound cooked, peeled small shrimp, thawed if frozen

½ teaspoon garam masala, plus extra to garnish

6 pooris, kept warm (see page 191)

fresh chopped cilantro, to garnish

1 Put the coriander seeds, peppercorns, garlic, turmeric, chili powder, and salt into a small food processor or spice grinder and blend to a thick paste. Alternatively, use a mortar and pestle.

2 Melt the ghee in a wok or large skillet over low–medium heat. Add the spice paste and cook, stirring constantly, for about 30 seconds.

3 Add the grated onion and stir for an additional 30 seconds. Stir in the tomatoes and sugar. Bring to a boil, stirring and mashing the tomatoes against the side of the pan to break them down, and simmer for 10 minutes, or until reduced. Taste and adjust the seasoning, adding extra salt, if needed.

4 Add the shrimp and sprinkle with the garam masala. When the shrimp are hot, arrange the warm pooris on plates and top each with a portion of shrimp. Sprinkle with the chopped cilantro and garam masala and serve immediately.

Jhinga masala vadas

MASALA SHRIMP CAKES

Perfect as canapés, these Goan-inspired shrimp cakes are packed with the punchy, fresh flavors of garlic, ginger, coconut, chile, cilantro, and mint. Squeeze a little fresh lime juice over them to add even more zing and serve with a refreshing chilled beverage.

MAKES: 20

PREP: 20 minutes, plus chilling time

COOK: 12–15 minutes

¼ cup vegetable oil or peanut oil
lime wedges, to serve

SHRIMP CAKES

1¾ pounds raw jumbo shrimp, peeled and deveined

2 fresh red chiles, seeded and minced

⅓ cup finely chopped fresh cilantro

⅓ cup finely chopped fresh mint

1 teaspoon coconut cream or coconut milk

4 scallions, finely sliced

2 garlic cloves, finely chopped

2 teaspoons finely grated fresh ginger

½ cup fresh white bread crumbs

2 teaspoons ground cumin

1 teaspoon chili powder

1 medium egg, lightly beaten

1. To make the shrimp cakes, coarsely chop the shrimp and put them into a food processor with the remaining ingredients. Blend to a coarse paste. Transfer the mixture to a bowl, cover, and chill in the refrigerator for at least 6–8 hours, or overnight.

2. Preheat the oven to 400°F. Line a baking sheet with parchment paper.

3. Shape the shrimp mixture into 20 small patties, about 1½ inches in diameter. Place on the prepared baking sheet and lightly brush with the oil. Bake in the preheated oven for 12–15 minutes, or until slightly puffed up and light golden.

4. Serve warm or at room temperature with lime wedges for squeezing over the top.

TIP
To make masala fish cakes, simply replace the shrimp with coarsely chopped white fish fillet (such as cod or halibut).

Samudrapheni masala

CRISPY SPICY SQUID

This quick-and-easy appetizer is inspired by the cuisine of the Konkan Coast, a rugged stretch of the coastline of western India rich in natural beauty. Serve these delectable morsels on their own or with steamed rice and a mild lentil curry or dal.

SERVES: 4

PREP: 20 minutes, plus marinating time

COOK: 10–12 minutes

1 pound prepared squid rings

⅓ cup semolina

⅓ cup cornstarch

vegetable oil or peanut oil, for deep-frying

MARINADE

3 fresh red chiles, finely chopped

2 teaspoons finely grated fresh ginger

3 garlic cloves, crushed

2 tablespoons white wine vinegar

¼ cup vegetable oil or peanut oil

1 teaspoon ground cumin

1 teaspoon crushed coriander seeds

1 teaspoon salt

1 Place all the marinade ingredients into a small food processor and blend until smooth. Transfer to a shallow, nonmetallic dish and add the squid rings. Toss to mix well, cover, and let marinate in the refrigerator for 1 hour.

2 In a separate bowl, mix together the semolina and cornflour. Set aside.

3 Heat enough oil for deep-frying in a large saucepan or deep fryer to 350–375°F, or until a cube of bread browns in 30 seconds. Remove the squid from its marinade and toss it in the semolina mixture to coat. Shake off any excess and deep-fry the squid, in batches, for 1–2 minutes, or until crisp and golden.

4 Remove the squid with a slotted spoon and drain on paper towels. Serve immediately.

TIP

For crispy spicy shrimp, replace the squid with raw, peeled and deveined jumbo shrimp.

Gosht hara kabab

CORIANDER LAMB KABOBS

These fragrant, subtly spiced kabobs are traditionally cooked in a tandoor oven to produce a dry exterior while keeping the center tender. Cooking them under a hot broiler or over glowing coals also gives good results.

MAKES: 6

PREP: 15–20 minutes, plus standing time

COOK: 5–7 minutes

1½ pounds fresh ground lamb

1 onion, grated

3 tablespoons finely chopped fresh cilantro, leaves and stems

3 tablespoons finely chopped fresh mint

3 tablespoons chickpea (besan) flour

1½ tablespoons ground almonds (almond meal)

1-inch piece fresh ginger, grated

3 tablespoons lemon juice

2 tablespoons plain yogurt

2 teaspoons ground cumin

2 teaspoons ground coriander

1½ teaspoons salt

1½ teaspoons garam masala

1 teaspoon ground cinnamon

½ teaspoon pepper

vegetable oil or peanut oil, for brushing

1 Put all the ingredients, except the oil, into a large bowl and use your hands to mix together until combined and smooth. Cover the bowl with plastic wrap and let stand at room temperature for about 45 minutes.

2 With wet hands, divide the lamb mixture into 24 equal balls. Thread four balls onto each of six metal skewers, leaving a little space between each one.

3 Preheat the broiler to high or light barbecue coals and let burn until they turn gray. Lightly brush the broiler rack or grill rack with oil. Add the skewers and cook, turning frequently, for 5–7 minutes, until the lamb is completely cooked through and there are no signs of pink when you pierce it with the tip of a sharp knife. Serve immediately.

Boti shashlik

MARINATED LAMB BROCHETTES

In this recipe, tender cubes of lamb are infused with a spiced yogurt marinade, skewered with red bell peppers and shallots, and broiled. Make sure to trim off any excess fat from the meat before cutting it into cubes.

MAKES: 4

PREP: 15–20 minutes, plus marinating time

COOK: 11–12 minutes, plus standing time

1½ pounds boned leg of lamb, cut into 1-inch cubes

2 tablespoons apple cider vinegar

½ teaspoon salt, or to taste

1 tablespoon garlic paste

1 tablespoon ginger paste

½ cup yogurt, strained, or Greek-style yogurt

1 tablespoon chickpea (besan) flour

1 teaspoon ground cumin

1 teaspoon garam masala

½–1 teaspoon chili powder

½ teaspoon ground turmeric

3 tablespoons vegetable oil or peanut oil, plus extra for brushing

½ red bell pepper, seeded and cut into 1-inch pieces

½ green bell pepper, seeded and cut into 1-inch pieces

8 shallots, halved

4 tablespoons butter, melted

1 Put the meat into a large, nonmetallic bowl and add the vinegar, salt, garlic paste, and ginger paste. Mix together thoroughly, cover, and let marinate in the refrigerator for 30 minutes.

2 Put the yogurt and chickpea flour into a separate bowl and beat together with a fork until smooth. Add the cumin, garam masala, chili powder, turmeric, and oil and mix together thoroughly. Add the yogurt mixture to the marinated meat, then add the bell peppers and shallots and stir until well blended. Cover and let marinate in the refrigerator for 2–3 hours, or overnight. Return to room temperature before cooking.

3 Preheat the broiler to high. Brush the broiler rack and four metal skewers with oil.

4 Thread the marinated lamb, bell peppers, and shallots alternately onto the prepared skewers. Place the skewers on the prepared broiler rack and cook under the preheated broiler for 4 minutes. Brush generously with half the melted butter and cook for an additional 2 minutes. Turn over and cook for 3–4 minutes. Brush with the remaining butter and cook for an additional 2 minutes.

5 Balance the brochettes over a large saucepan or skillet and let stand for 5–6 minutes before sliding off the skewers with a knife. Serve immediately.

Kathi roll

CHICKEN & EGG ROLLS

In Bengal, these egg-based pancakes are served as street-side snacks. They can be filled with spiced vegetables, paneer, or meat—here, they are stuffed with marinated, broiled chicken. For extra zing, add a couple of tablespoons of cilantro chutney (see page 40) to the filling.

MAKES: 6

PREP: 30 minutes, plus marinating time

COOK: 25–30 minutes

2 skinless, boneless chicken breasts, cut into bite-size pieces

1⅔ cups all-purpose flour, plus extra for dusting

1 teaspoon salt

1 tablespoon vegetable oil or peanut oil

½ cup milk

4 eggs

fresh mint leaves and sliced red onion, to serve

MARINADE

2 garlic cloves, crushed

1 teaspoon grated fresh ginger

2 teaspoons ground cumin

1 teaspoon chili powder

¼ teaspoon ground turmeric

¼ teaspoon garam masala

2 teaspoons tomato paste

2 tablespoons plain yogurt

1 tablespoon lemon juice

1 teaspoon salt

1 tablespoon vegetable oil or peanut oil

1 Put all the marinade ingredients into a nonmetallic bowl with the chicken and stir to mix well. Cover and chill in the refrigerator for 6–8 hours, or overnight, if possible.

2 When ready to cook, preheat the broiler to medium–high. Thread the marinated chicken onto metal skewers. Put the chicken skewers onto a broiler rack and cook under the preheated broiler, turning once, for 12–15 minutes, until cooked through and tender. Remove the chicken from the skewers and keep warm.

3 Meanwhile, sift the flour and salt into a large bowl. Add the oil, milk, and one of the eggs and knead for 8–10 minutes, until smooth. Form into a ball, cover, and let rest for 15–20 minutes.

4 Divide the dough into six equal pieces and form each into a ball. On a lightly floured surface, roll each ball into a circle that is 6¼–6½ inches in diameter and about ⅛ inch thick. Lightly beat the remaining eggs.

5 Heat a nonstick skillet over medium heat. Working one at a time, place a dough circle in the pan and cook for 1 minute. Flip it over and spread 1 tablespoon of the beaten egg all over the surface. Immediately flip it over again and cook for 30–40 seconds, then remove from the heat. Repeat until all the dough circles have been cooked.

6 Divide the chicken among the egg rolls and sprinkle with a few mint leaves and some sliced red onion. Roll tightly to enclose the filling and serve immediately.

Murgh momo

STEAMED CHICKEN DUMPLINGS

Especially popular in Darjeeling (the hill station in West Bengal), these steamed stuffed chicken dumplings are an example of the Nepalese and Tibetan influences on Indian cuisine as a result of the close proximity between these two countries.

MAKES: 20

PREP: 30 minutes, plus marinating & resting time

COOK: 12–15 minutes

1 tablespoon white wine vinegar

1 tablespoon dark soy sauce

6 scallions, minced

2 garlic cloves, crushed

2 teaspoons salt

2 fresh green chiles, finely chopped

8 ounces fresh ground chicken

1¼ cups all-purpose flour, plus extra for dusting

⅓ cup lukewarm water

2 tablespoons vegetable oil or peanut oil, plus extra for brushing

sweet chili sauce, to serve

1 Mix together the vinegar, soy sauce, scallions, garlic, 1 teaspoon of the salt, and the chiles in a bowl. Add the ground chicken and, using your fingers, mix until well combined. Cover and let marinate for 30 minutes.

2 Meanwhile, sift the flour and the remaining salt into a large bowl. Add the water and oil and knead for 8–10 minutes to make a soft dough. Cover and let rest for 15–20 minutes.

3 Divide the dough into 20 small balls. On a lightly floured surface, roll each ball out into a thin circle that is 4 inches in diameter and about ¼ inch thick.

4 Place a little of the chicken mixture in the center of each dough circle. Fold in half to make a semicircular dumpling, sealing it tightly by carefully pinching together the folded edges.

5 Place the dumplings in a single layer in a steamer and lightly brush with oil. Steam over high heat for 12–15 minutes, or until the chicken is cooked through. Serve warm with sweet chili sauce.

TIP

You can make these dumplings up to a day in advance and steam them when you are ready to serve.

CHAPTER 3
MAIN DISHES

Thukpa

VEGETABLE NOODLE BROTH

This hearty vegetarian version of a popular noodle-based broth is another example of the influence of Tibetan cuisine in the Bengal region. It is a favorite among students and is served in many school and college cafeterias.

SERVES: 4

PREP: 20–25 minutes

COOK: 25–30 minutes

1 pound dried thick egg noodles

2 tablespoons vegetable oil or peanut oil

1 onion, finely chopped

1 teaspoon ground cumin

½ teaspoon ground turmeric

2 garlic cloves, crushed

2 teaspoons grated fresh ginger

1 teaspoon salt

2 fresh green chiles, finely chopped

1 cup thinly sliced snow peas (sliced lengthwise)

2 large carrots, cut into matchsticks

1 red bell pepper, seeded and thinly sliced

2 tomatoes, finely chopped

2 tablespoons dark soy sauce

4 cups vegetable broth

1 teaspoon pepper

1 (6-ounce) package baby spinach

⅓ cup finely chopped fresh cilantro

1 teaspoon toasted sesame oil

1 Cook the noodles according to the package directions. Drain, rinse with cold water, and set aside.

2 Meanwhile, heat the vegetable oil in a large saucepan over medium heat, add the onion, and sauté for 8–10 minutes, or until lightly browned.

3 Add the cumin, turmeric, garlic, ginger, salt, and chiles to the pan and sauté for 1–2 minutes. Add the snow peas, carrots, and red bell pepper and sauté for an additional 1–2 minutes.

4 Add the tomatoes, soy sauce, broth, and pepper. Bring to a boil, then reduce the heat and simmer for 10–12 minutes, until the vegetables are tender.

5 Add the reserved noodles and the spinach and bring back to a boil. Stir until the spinach wilts, then remove from the heat and stir in the chopped cilantro and sesame oil. Ladle into bowls and serve immediately.

Shukto

BENGALI VEGETABLE CURRY

A traditional Bengali curry, *shukto* uses a mixture of vegetables and is cooked with a mustard seed-and-white poppy seed paste. *Panch phoran* is a Bengali spice mixture made up of equal quantities of fenugreek seeds, fennel seeds, mustard seeds, nigella seeds, and cumin seeds; it is available in Indian grocery stores and online.

SERVES: 4

PREP: 30 minutes, plus soaking time

COOK: 25–30 minutes

⅓ cup white poppy seeds (khus khus)

3 tablespoons black mustard seeds

2 teaspoons grated fresh ginger

¼ cup vegetable oil or peanut oil

2 fresh green chiles, split lengthwise

1 tablespoon panch phoran or curry powder

2 cups ½-inch fresh bitter melon (kerala or balsam pear) cubes

2 Yukon gold or russet potatoes, peeled and cut into ½-inch cubes

1 eggplant, cut into ½-inch cubes

1 zucchini, cut into ½-inch cubes

1 carrot, cut into ½-inch cubes

1 tomato, finely chopped

⅔ cup fresh or frozen peas

1¾ cups cold water

¼ teaspoon ground turmeric

2 teaspoons salt

1 teaspoon palm sugar or packed light brown sugar

½ cup milk

1. Soak the white poppy seeds and 2 tablespoons of the mustard seeds in warm water for 1 hour. Drain and blend with the ginger to make a paste.

2. Heat the oil in a large skillet and add the remaining mustard seeds and the chiles. When the mustard seeds start to pop, add the panch phoran, the melon and all the vegetables. Add half the water and stir to mix well, then cover tightly and cook, stirring frequently, over medium heat for 10–12 minutes.

3. Add half the white poppy seed-and-mustard seed paste, the turmeric, and salt. Add the remaining water and cook, stirring frequently, over low–medium heat for an additional 10–15 minutes.

4. Add the remaining white poppy seed-and-mustard seed paste, the palm sugar, and milk and cook for an additional 5 minutes, or until the vegetables are tender. Serve hot.

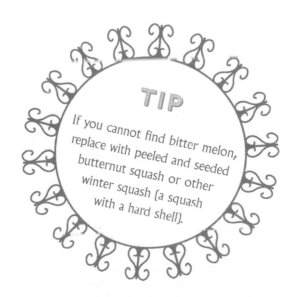

TIP

If you cannot find bitter melon, replace with peeled and seeded butternut squash or other winter squash (a squash with a hard shell).

Sambhar

SOUTH INDIAN LENTIL & VEGETABLE CURRY

This light, soup-like lentil curry from Tamil Nadu is probably the most typical dish of south India. With a large vegetarian population in the region, most people will eat one version or another of this every day.

SERVES: 4–6

1 cup split red lentils (masoor dal), rinsed

6 ounces new potatoes, scrubbed and finely diced

1 large carrot, finely diced

1 green bell pepper, seeded and finely chopped

4 cups cold water

¼ teaspoon ground turmeric

¼ teaspoon asafetida or garlic powder

1 tablespoon tamarind paste

2 teaspoons sambhar masala, or to taste (see page 29)

salt, to taste

GARNISH

1½ tablespoons vegetable or peanut oil

12 fresh curry leaves

2 dried red chiles

1 teaspoon black mustard seeds

PREP: 15–20 minutes, plus soaking time

1 Put the red lentils into a bowl with enough water to cover and let soak for 30 minutes, changing the water once.

2 Drain the lentils. Put them into a wok or large skillet with the potatoes, carrot, and green bell pepper and pour the water over the vegetables. Bring to a boil, skimming the surface as necessary. Reduce the heat to the lowest setting, stir in the turmeric and asafetida, and partly cover the pan. Simmer, stirring occasionally, for 15–20 minutes, until the vegetables and lentils are tender but the lentils aren't falling apart.

COOK: 30–35 minutes

3 Stir in the tamarind paste and sambhar masala. Taste and adjust the seasoning, adding extra masala and salt, if desired. Continue simmering slowly while making the garnish.

4 To make the garnish, heat the oil in a large saucepan over high heat. Add the curry leaves, chiles, and mustard seeds and stir quickly, being careful to stand back because they will splatter. Transfer the lentil mixture to a serving dish and pour the hot oil and spices over them. Serve immediately.

Mattar paneer

PEAS & PANEER IN SPICY TOMATO SAUCE

In this vegetable dish from northern India, tender morsels of paneer are simmered in a spice-infused tomato sauce. Paneer is a great source of protein for people who don't eat meat.

SERVES: 4

PREP: 10–15 minutes

COOK: 30–35 minutes

¼ cup vegetable oil or peanut oil

8 ounces paneer or tofu, cut into 1-inch cubes

4 green cardamom pods, bruised

2 bay leaves

1 onion, finely chopped

2 teaspoons garlic paste

2 teaspoons ginger paste

2 teaspoons ground coriander

½ teaspoon ground turmeric

½–1 teaspoon chili powder

⅔ cup canned diced tomatoes

2 cups warm water

1 teaspoon salt, or to taste

1 cup frozen peas

½ teaspoon garam masala

2 tablespoons light cream

2 tablespoons chopped fresh cilantro

1 Heat 2 tablespoons of the oil in a nonstick saucepan over medium heat. Add the paneer and cook, stirring frequently, for 3–4 minutes, or until evenly browned. Remove the paneer from the pan and drain on paper towels. Set aside.

2 Add the remaining oil to the pan and reduce the heat to low. Add the cardamom pods and bay leaves and let sizzle gently for 20–25 seconds. Add the onion, increase the heat to medium, and cook, stirring frequently, for 4–5 minutes, until the onion is soft. Add the garlic and ginger pastes and cook, stirring frequently, until the onion is a pale-golden color.

3 Add the ground coriander, turmeric, and chili powder and cook, stirring, for 1 minute. Add the tomatoes and cook, stirring, for 4–5 minutes. Add 2 tablespoons of the water and cook, stirring, for 3 minutes, or until the oil separates from the spice paste.

4 Add the remaining water and the salt. Bring to a boil, then simmer, uncovered, for 7–8 minutes. Add the reserved paneer and the peas and simmer for 5 minutes. Stir in the garam masala, cream, and chopped cilantro, then remove from the heat. Serve immediately.

Aloo gobhi

GARLIC & CHILE-FLAVORED POTATOES WITH CAULIFLOWER

This well-known and popular Indian dish always contains potatoes and cauliflower, but other ingredients can vary—there are as many different versions as there are cooks. This recipe is easy to make, can be partly prepared ahead (up to step 2), and tastes delicious.

SERVES: 4

12 ounces new potatoes

1 small cauliflower

2 tablespoons vegetable oil or peanut oil

1 teaspoon black or brown mustard seeds

1 teaspoon cumin seeds

5 large garlic cloves, lightly crushed, then chopped

1–2 fresh green chiles, finely chopped (seeded, if desired)

½ teaspoon ground turmeric

½ teaspoon salt, or to taste

2 tablespoons chopped fresh cilantro

PREP: 10 minutes, plus soaking time

1 Cook the potatoes in their skins in a saucepan of boiling water for 20 minutes, or until tender. Drain, then soak in cold water for 30 minutes. Peel them, if desired, then halve or quarter according to their size—they should be only slightly bigger than the size of the cauliflower florets.

2 Meanwhile, divide the cauliflower into small florets and blanch in a large saucepan of boiling salted water for 3 minutes. Drain and plunge into ice water to prevent additional cooking, then drain again.

3 Heat the oil in a saucepan over medium heat. When hot, but not smoking, add the mustard seeds, then the cumin seeds. Remove from the heat and add the garlic and chiles. Return to a low heat and cook, stirring, until the garlic has a light-brown tinge.

COOK: 30 minutes

4 Stir in the turmeric, followed by the cauliflower and the potatoes. Add the salt, increase the heat slightly, and cook, stirring, until the vegetables are well blended with the spices and heated through.

5 Stir in the chopped cilantro, remove from the heat, and serve immediately.

Baingan ka bharta

SPICED MASHED EGGPLANT

The word *bharta* (pronounced "bhurr-taaah") refers to dishes in which the ingredients are coarsely mashed either before or after the dish is prepared. Bhartas are largely north Indian in origin and can be made from all kinds of vegetables. This version of *baingan ka bharta* has its origins in the Punjab.

SERVES: 4

PREP: 15–20 minutes

COOK: 45–55 minutes

4 large eggplant

2 tablespoons vegetable oil or peanut oil

4 tablespoons butter

2 onions, finely chopped

2 teaspoons grated fresh ginger

4 garlic cloves, crushed

2 fresh green chiles, finely sliced

3 tomatoes, finely chopped

2 teaspoons salt

1 teaspoon chili powder

1 teaspoon smoked paprika

2 teaspoons ground coriander

1 teaspoon ground cumin

1 teaspoon ground turmeric

½ teaspoon garam masala

⅓ cup finely chopped fresh cilantro

1 Prick the eggplant all over with a fork and roast them over an open flame (if you have a gas stove) or under a medium–hot broiler, turning them from time to time, for 20–25 minutes, until the skin blackens and chars. To check if the eggplant are cooked, press the back of a spoon into the skin; if it enters the eggplant like soft butter, it is done. Let cool.

2 When the eggplant are cool enough to handle, remove the skins and coarsely mash the pulp. Set aside.

3 Heat the oil and butter in a large, nonstick skillet and add the onions. Sauté for 5–6 minutes, until softened. Add the ginger, garlic, and chiles and sauté for 1–2 minutes.

4 Stir in the tomatoes and salt and cook for 12–15 minutes. Add the chili powder, paprika, ground coriander, ground cumin, and turmeric.

5 Stir in the reserved eggplant flesh and cook for 3–4 minutes. Stir in the garam masala and chopped cilantro. Serve immediately.

TIP

If cooking the eggplant on the stove, it is a good idea to line the bottom of the burner with aluminum foil to make it easy to clean later on.

Mumbai aloo

BOMBAY POTATOES

This simple dish of spiced potatoes is easy to make and goes with almost anything. Any leftovers can be wrapped up in a chapati for a quick lunch or snack the next day.

SERVES: 6

PREP: 10 minutes

COOK: 30 minutes

1 pound new potatoes, halved

1 teaspoon ground turmeric

pinch of salt

¼ cup ghee or vegetable oil or peanut oil

6 fresh curry leaves

1 dried red chile

2 fresh green chiles, chopped

½ teaspoon nigella seeds

1 teaspoon black mustard seeds

½ teaspoon cumin seeds

½ teaspoon fennel seeds

¼ teaspoon asafetida or garlic powder

2 onions, chopped

⅓ cup chopped fresh cilantro

juice of ½ lime

1 Put the potatoes into a large, heavy saucepan and pour in just enough cold water to cover. Add ½ teaspoon of the turmeric and the salt and bring to a boil. Simmer for 10 minutes, or until tender. Drain and set aside.

2 Heat the ghee in a large, heavy skillet. Add the curry leaves and dried red chile and cook, stirring frequently, for a few minutes, or until the chile is blackened.

3 Add the remaining turmeric, the green chiles, nigella seeds, mustard seeds, cumin seeds, fennel seeds, asafetida, onions, and chopped cilantro. Cook, stirring constantly, for 5 minutes, or until the onions have softened.

4 Stir in the reserved potatoes and cook over low heat, stirring frequently, for 10 minutes, or until heated through. Squeeze the lime juice over the potatoes and serve immediately.

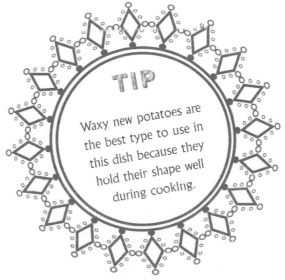

TIP

Waxy new potatoes are the best type to use in this dish because they hold their shape well during cooking.

Bhindi-pyaaz

OKRA STIR-FRIED WITH ONIONS

Bhindi, or okra, is a versatile vegetable. The combination of the soft, green okra, bright-red bell pepper, and white onion in this dish, all dotted with dark mustard seeds, creates a feast for the eyes.

SERVES: 4

PREP: 15 minutes

COOK: 10 minutes

10 ounces okra

1 small red bell pepper

1 onion

2 tablespoons vegetable oil or peanut oil

1 teaspoon black or brown mustard seeds

½ teaspoon cumin seeds

3 large garlic cloves, lightly crushed, then chopped

½ teaspoon chili powder

½ teaspoon salt, or to taste

½ teaspoon garam masala

1 Scrub each piece of okra gently, rinse well in cold running water, then slice off the hard head. Halve diagonally and set aside.

2 Remove the seeds and core from the red bell pepper and cut into 1½-inch strips. Halve the onion lengthwise and cut into ¼-inch-thick slices. Set aside.

3 Heat the oil in a heavy skillet or wok over medium heat. When hot, but not smoking, add the mustard seeds, followed by the cumin seeds. Remove from the heat and add the garlic. Return to low heat and cook the garlic gently, stirring, for 1 minute, or until lightly browned.

4 Add the reserved okra, red bell pepper, and onion, increase the heat to medium–high, and sauté for 2 minutes. Add the chili powder and salt and sauté for an additional 3 minutes. Add the garam masala and sauté for 1 minute. Remove from the heat and serve immediately.

TIP

To test the oil temperature in step 3, drop in a couple of mustard seeds—they should pop immediately.

Bharwan baigan tamattari

TOMATO-STUFFED EGGPLANT

From Maharashtra, this is a technique for cooking whole, small eggplant with a thin layer of spicy stuffing between the slices. It is an excellent dish for entertaining because the fussy work can be done well in advance.

MAKES: 4

PREP: 20–30 minutes

COOK: 30–35 minutes

4 small eggplant, about 5 inches long

vegetable oil or peanut oil, for pan-frying

STUFFING

4 firm tomatoes, grated

2 onions, grated

2 fresh red chiles, chopped (seeded, if desired)

¼ cup lemon juice

¼ cup finely chopped fresh cilantro

1½ teaspoons garlic paste

1½ teaspoons ginger paste

1½ tablespoons ground coriander

2 teaspoons ground cumin

1 teaspoon fennel seeds

1 teaspoon ground turmeric

1 teaspoon salt

1 tablespoon chickpea (besan) flour (if needed)

1 To make the stuffing, mix together the tomatoes, onions, chiles, lemon juice, chopped cilantro, garlic paste, ginger paste, ground coriander, ground cumin, fennel seeds, turmeric, and salt in a nonmetallic bowl. The filling should not be stiff, but thick enough that it doesn't slide off the eggplant slices. If the tomatoes are juicy and have made the filling too runny, gradually stir in the chickpea flour.

2 To prepare the eggplant, work with one at a time. Slit lengthwise into four parallel slices without cutting through the stem end, so that the eggplant remains in one piece. Lightly fan the slices apart, then use a small spoon or your fingers to fill, dividing one-quarter of the stuffing among the slices and covering each slice to the edges. Carefully layer the slices back into position so the eggplant looks whole again. Repeat this process with the remaining eggplant.

3 Choose a heavy skillet with a tight-fitting lid—it needs to be large enough to hold the eggplant in a single layer. Heat enough oil to cover the bottom of the pan with a layer about ¼ inch deep, then add the eggplant in a single layer.

4 Put the pan over the lowest heat and cover tightly. Let cook for 15 minutes, then carefully turn the eggplant over. Replace the cover on the pan and continue cooking for an additional 10–15 minutes, or until the eggplant are tender when you pierce them with the tip of a sharp knife. Check occasionally while the eggplant are cooking; and, if they start to stick to the bottom of the pan, stir in a couple of tablespoons of water. Serve hot or at room temperature.

Tandoori khumbi

TANDOORI MUSHROOM CURRY

This north Indian mushroom curry makes for great vegetarian entertaining. If desired, you can replace the peas with chopped spinach for a tasty variation. Serve hot with cooked basmati rice or warm chapatis.

SERVES: 4

PREP: 15–20 minutes

COOK: 35 minutes

2 tablespoons vegetable oil or peanut oil

1 teaspoon cumin seeds

1 teaspoon coriander seeds

1 onion, finely chopped

2 teaspoons ground coriander

1 teaspoon ground cumin

6 black peppercorns

½ teaspoon freshly ground cardamom seeds

1 teaspoon ground turmeric

1 tablespoon tandoori masala (see page 29)

1 fresh red chile, finely chopped

2 garlic cloves, crushed

2 teaspoons grated fresh ginger

1 (28-ounce) can diced tomatoes

1¼ pounds cremini or white button mushrooms, halved or thickly sliced

2 teaspoon salt

1⅓ cups fresh or frozen peas

¼ cup coarsely chopped fresh cilantro

⅓ cup light cream

1 Heat the oil in a large saucepan over medium heat. Add the cumin seeds and coriander seeds and cook for 1 minute, or until sizzling.

2 Add the onion, ground coriander, cumin, peppercorns, ground cardamom seeds, turmeric, tandoori masala, chile, garlic, and ginger. Cook, stirring, for 2–3 minutes, or until the onion is soft and the mixture is aromatic.

3 Add the tomatoes, mushrooms, and salt. Stir until well combined. Bring to a boil, then reduce the heat to low and cook, uncovered, for 25 minutes.

4 Add the peas and stir to mix well. Cook for an additional 4–5 minutes, or until piping hot.

5 Remove from the heat, sprinkle with the cilantro, and drizzle with the cream. Stir to mix well. Serve immediately.

Patrani macchi

PARSI-STYLE BAKED FISH WRAPPED IN BANANA LEAVES

This delicious Parsi-style baked fish dish, from the western shores of India, looks pretty when served wrapped up in banana leaves. Your guests will enjoy the mouthwatering aromas that are released as they unwrap their individual packages at the table.

SERVES: 4

PREP: 15–20 minutes

COOK: 15–20 minutes

4 thick cod fillets (about 7 ounces each), skinned

2 teaspoons ground turmeric

1 large fresh banana leaf

SPICE PASTE

2 teaspoons ground cumin

2 teaspoons ground coriander

1½ teaspoons palm sugar or packed light brown sugar

1 cup coconut cream or coconut milk

4 fresh red chiles, seeded and chopped

2½ cups chopped fresh cilantro

¼ cup chopped fresh mint

5 garlic cloves, chopped

1 teaspoon finely grated fresh ginger

¼ cup vegetable oil or peanut oil

juice of 2 limes

2 teaspoons salt

1 Preheat the oven to 400°F.

2 Place the fish fillets in a single layer on a plate and sprinkle with the turmeric. Rub into the fish and set aside.

3 Put the ingredients for the spice paste into a food processor and process until fairly smooth. Set aside.

4 Cut the banana leaf into four 9½-inch squares. Soften the banana leaf squares by dipping them into a saucepan of hot water for a few seconds. Once the banana leaf squares have become pliant, wipe them dry with paper towels and arrange on a work surface

5 Apply the spice paste liberally to both sides of each piece of fish. Place a piece of fish on top of each banana leaf square and wrap up like a package, securing with bamboo skewers or string.

6 Place the packages on a baking sheet and bake in the preheated oven for 15–20 minutes, until cooked through. Transfer to plates and serve immediately.

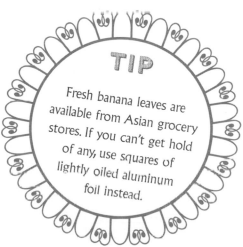

TIP

Fresh banana leaves are available from Asian grocery stores. If you can't get hold of any, use squares of lightly oiled aluminum foil instead.

Kaalvan

MAHARASHTRIAN SALMON CURRY

This simple fish curry is packed with flavor. *Kaalvan* is the Maharashtrian term for any sauce-based fish dish. You can use any firm fish fillet or fish steaks instead of the salmon, if desired. Serve with freshly cooked basmati rice to soak up the delicious cooking liquid.

SERVES: 4

PREP: 5–10 minutes

COOK: 15–20 minutes

⅓ cup vegetable oil or peanut oil

8 salmon steaks (about 5½ ounces each)

2 teaspoons cornstarch

1 teaspoon hot chili powder

1 teaspoon paprika

½ teaspoon ground turmeric

2 teaspoons ground cumin

1 teaspoon ground coriander

2 teaspoons salt

1 teaspoon tamarind paste

1¾ cups coconut milk

1¾ cups cold water

1 Heat the oil in a nonstick saucepan and add the fish. Cook the salmon for 1–2 minutes on each side.

2 Mix together the cornstarch, spices, salt, tamarind paste, and coconut milk. Pour this mixture into the saucepan with the water.

3 Bring to a boil, then reduce the heat, cover, and cook gently for 10–12 minutes, or until the fish is cooked through and the sauce has thickened slightly (it should still be runny). Serve immediately.

Goa che nalla chi kadi

GOAN-STYLE SEAFOOD CURRY

With mustard seeds, curry leaves, and a creamy coconut sauce, this quick-and-easy dish could have originated anywhere in southern India, not just in tropical Goa on the west coast.

SERVES: 4–6

PREP: 15 minutes

COOK: 20 minutes

3 tablespoons vegetable oil or peanut oil

1 tablespoon black mustard seeds

12 fresh curry leaves

6 shallots, finely chopped

1 garlic clove, crushed

1 teaspoon ground turmeric

½ teaspoon ground coriander

¼–½ teaspoon chili powder

1¼ cups coconut milk

1 pound skinless, boneless white fish, such as monkfish, halibut, or cod, cut into large chunks

1 pound large raw shrimp, peeled and deveined

juice and finely grated zest of 1 lime

salt, to taste

1 Heat the oil in a wok or large skillet over high heat. Add the mustard seeds and stir them around for about 1 minute, or until they start to pop. Stir in the curry leaves.

2 Add the shallots and garlic and sauté for about 5 minutes, or until the shallots are golden. Stir in the turmeric, ground coriander, and chili powder and continue sautéing for about 30 seconds. Add the coconut milk. Bring to a boil, then reduce the heat to medium and stir for about 2 minutes.

3 Reduce the heat to low, add the fish, and simmer for 1 minute, spooning the sauce over the fish and gently stirring it around. Add the shrimp and continue to simmer for an additional 4–5 minutes, until the fish flakes easily and the shrimp curl and turn pink.

4 Add half the lime juice, then taste and add more lime juice and salt, if desired. Sprinkle with the lime zest and serve immediately.

TIP

You can use coconut cream in place of coconut milk, but don't confuse it with cream of coconut, the sweetened version used for making cocktails and other drinks.

Macchi masala

BALTI FISH CURRY

This dish is one for those who prefer robustly flavored dishes, such as the ones served in northern India, to the coconut-based ones of the south. It is particularly tasty when served with any Indian bread.

SERVES: 4–6

PREP: 10–15 minutes, plus marinating time

COOK: 15–20 minutes

2 pounds thick white fish fillets, such as monkfish, cod, or halibut, cut into large chunks

⅔ cup ghee or vegetable oil or peanut oil

2 large onions, chopped

1½ teaspoons salt

⅔ cup cold water

chopped fresh cilantro, to garnish

MARINADE

¾ teaspoon garlic paste

¾ teaspoon ginger paste

1 fresh green chile, seeded and chopped

1 teaspoon ground coriander

1 teaspoon ground cumin

½ teaspoon ground turmeric

¼–½ teaspoon chili powder

pinch of salt

1 tablespoon cold water

2 bay leaves, torn

1 To make the marinade, mix together the garlic and ginger pastes, green chile, ground coriander, cumin, turmeric, chili powder, and salt in a large bowl. Gradually stir in the water to form a thin paste.

2 Add the fish chunks to the marinade and toss gently to coat with the spice mixture. Tuck the bay leaves underneath and let marinate in the refrigerator for at least 30 minutes, or up to 4 hours.

3 Remove the fish from the refrigerator 15 minutes in advance of cooking. Melt the ghee in a large skillet or wok over medium–high heat. Add the onions, sprinkle with the salt, and cook, stirring frequently, for 8 minutes, or until the onions are soft and golden.

4 Gently add the fish with its marinade to the pan and stir in the water. Bring to a boil, then immediately reduce the heat and cook, spooning the sauce over the fish and stirring gently, for 4–5 minutes, until the fish is cooked through and the flesh flakes easily. Garnish with chopped cilantro and serve immediately.

Doi mach
SOLE IN SPICY YOGURT SAUCE

This dish is typical of the cuisine of the Bengal region, where seafood is an important part of the everyday diet. It can also be made using butterfish, one of the jewels of Indian seafood cooking, or flounder. Freshly cooked okra would make a delicious accompaniment.

SERVES: 4   **PREP:** 15–20 minutes   **COOK:** 20–25 minutes

2 tablespoons vegetable oil or peanut oil

1 large onion, sliced

1½-inch piece fresh ginger, finely chopped

½ teaspoon salt

¼ teaspoon ground turmeric

pinch of ground cinnamon

pinch of ground cloves

1 cup plain yogurt

1 tablespoon all-purpose flour

small pinch of chili powder

4 skinless sole fillets (about 5½ ounces each), wiped dry

2 tablespoons ghee or vegetable oil or peanut oil

salt and pepper, to taste

sliced fresh green chiles, to garnish

1 Heat the oil in a large skillet over medium–high heat. Add the onion and sauté for about 8 minutes, or until it is soft and dark golden brown. Add the ginger and stir for an additional minute.

2 Add the salt, turmeric, cinnamon, and cloves and sauté for an additional 30 seconds. Remove the pan from the heat and stir in the yogurt, a little at a time, beating constantly.

3 Transfer the yogurt mixture to a blender or food processor and process until a paste forms.

4 Season the flour with the chili powder and salt and pepper. Spread out the seasoned flour on a plate and use to dust the fish fillets lightly on both sides.

5 Wipe out the skillet with paper towels, then melt the ghee over medium–high heat. When it is bubbling, reduce the heat to medium and add the fish fillets in a single layer. Cook for 2½ minutes, or until golden.

6 Turn the fish fillets over and continue cooking for an additional minute. Add the yogurt sauce to the pan and reheat, stirring, until the sauce is hot, the fish is cooked through, and the flesh flakes easily. Transfer to plates, garnish with green chile, and serve immediately.

Macher jhol

BENGALI FISH CURRY

Cooking with mustard-flavored oil, as in this dish, is common in the Bengal region. You can reduce the amount of mustard powder if you prefer a milder flavor, or replace with chile-infused olive oil if you want to increase the heat.

SERVES: 4

PREP: 15 minutes

COOK: 25–30 minutes

2 teaspoons coriander seeds

1 teaspoon cumin seeds

¼ cup peanut oil combined with 2 teaspoons dry mustard

1¾ pounds monkfish fillets, cut into large, bite-size pieces

2 potatoes, cut into finger-thick sticks

1 teaspoon ground turmeric

2 teaspoons salt

5 fresh green chiles, slit lengthwise

1 tablespoon panch phoran or curry powder

3⅔ cups cold water

cooked basmati rice, to serve

1 Dry-fry the coriander seeds and cumin seeds in a small skillet for 1–2 minutes. Remove the seeds from the pan and let cool, then finely grind in a spice grinder (or use a mortar and pestle). Set aside.

2 Heat 2 tablespoons of the peanut oil and dry mustard in a heavy saucepan until it just reaches smoking point. Remove from the heat and let cool, then heat up the oil again over medium heat. Add the fish and cook for a minute on each side. Remove with a slotted spoon and set aside.

3 Heat the remaining oil in the pan, add the potatoes, and sauté for 2–3 minutes. Add the turmeric, salt, chiles, panch phoran, and the reserved ground spices and sauté for 1 minute.

4 Pour in the water and bring to a boil. Reduce the heat and simmer for 12–15 minutes, or until the potatoes are just tender. Add the fish to the saucepan and simmer for 3–4 minutes, or until the fish is cooked through and the flesh flakes easily. Serve immediately with cooked basmati rice.

Paatrani macchi

STEAMED FISH WITH CILANTRO CHUTNEY

South Indian food is often served on glossy, dark-green banana leaves. Here, the leaves are wrapped around fish fillets with a fresh-tasting chutney to keep the fish moist while it cooks.

SERVES: 4

PREP: 10–15 minutes

COOK: 15 minutes

1 large fresh banana leaf

vegetable oil or peanut oil, for brushing

4 white fish fillets, such as pomfret, sole, or flounder (about 5 ounces) each

1 quantity of cilantro chutney (see page 40)

salt and pepper, to taste

lemon wedges, to serve

1 Cut the banana leaf into four squares, each large enough to fold around a fish fillet to make a tight package. Working with one banana leaf square at a time, lightly brush one side with oil. Put one of the fish fillets in the center of the oiled side, flesh side up. Spread one-quarter of the cilantro chutney over the top and season to taste with salt and pepper.

2 Wrap up the banana leaf square like a package, securing with bamboo skewers or string. Repeat with the remaining ingredients and banana leaf squares.

3 Place in a steamer large enough to hold the package in a single layer over a saucepan of boiling water. Add the fish, cover the pan, and steam for 15 minutes, or until the fish is cooked through and the flesh flakes easily. Transfer the fish packages to plates and serve with lemon wedges for squeezing over the fish.

TIP

To make the banana leaves easier to fold, briefly dip them in a saucepan of hot water until pliable. Dry thoroughly before using.

Tissario kadugu

MUSSELS WITH MUSTARD SEEDS & SHALLOTS

Baskets piled high with fresh mussels are a common sight along India's southern Malabar coast, and quickly cooked, fragrant dishes such as this are typical of those served in the local open-air harborside restaurants.

SERVES: 4

PREP: 5–10 minutes

COOK: 10–12 minutes

4½ pounds live mussels, scrubbed and debearded

3 tablespoons vegetable oil or peanut oil

1½ teaspoons black mustard seeds

8 shallots, chopped

2 garlic cloves, crushed

2 tablespoons white wine vinegar

4 small fresh red chiles

1¼ cups coconut cream or coconut milk

10 fresh curry leaves

½ teaspoon ground turmeric

¼–½ teaspoon chili powder

pinch of salt, or to taste

1 Discard any mussels with broken shells and any that refuse to close when tapped with a knife. Set the remainder aside.

2 Heat the oil in a large skillet or wok over medium–high heat. Add the mustard seeds and stir them around for about 1 minute, or until they start to pop.

3 Add the shallots and garlic and cook, stirring frequently, for 3 minutes, or until they start to brown. Stir in the vinegar, whole chiles, coconut cream, curry leaves, turmeric, chili powder, and salt and bring to a boil, stirring.

4 Reduce the heat to low. Add the reserved mussels, cover the pan, and let simmer, shaking the pan frequently, for 3–4 minutes, or until they are all open. Discard any mussels that remain closed. Ladle the mussels into deep bowls, then taste the broth and adjust the seasoning, adding extra salt, if desired. Spoon the broth over the mussels and serve immediately.

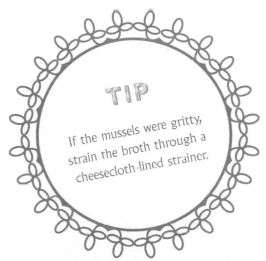

TIP

If the mussels were gritty, strain the broth through a cheesecloth-lined strainer.

Meen moilee

SOUTH INDIAN COCONUT FISH CURRY

This lightly spiced fish-and-coconut dish from the coastal region of Kerala combines fresh ingredients in a simple but effective way. It is a prime example of India's minimalist cooking with maximum flavor. Serve with freshly cooked basmati rice.

SERVES: 4

PREP: 10 minutes

COOK: 30–35 minutes

2 teaspoons salt

2 teaspoons ground turmeric

4 halibut fillets or steaks (about 7 ounces each)

2 tablespoons vegetable oil or peanut oil

2 onions, finely sliced

4 fresh green chiles, slit lengthwise

3 garlic cloves, thinly sliced

12 fresh curry leaves

1¾ cups coconut milk

¼ cup finely chopped fresh cilantro

1 Mix a teaspoon of the salt with a teaspoon of the turmeric. Gently rub into the fish fillets and set aside for 10–12 minutes.

2 Meanwhile, heat the oil in a skillet. Add the onions, chiles, and garlic and sauté for a few minutes. Add the curry leaves and continue to cook over low–medium heat for 12–15 minutes, or until the onion is translucent.

3 Add the remaining turmeric and salt to the pan. Pour in the coconut milk and bring to a simmer.

4 Add the fish, in a single layer, and simmer gently for 5–6 minutes, or until just cooked through.

5 Remove from the heat and sprinkle with the chopped cilantro. Serve immediately.

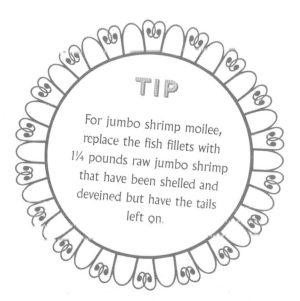

TIP

For jumbo shrimp moilee, replace the fish fillets with 1¼ pounds raw jumbo shrimp that have been shelled and deveined but have the tails left on.

Tamatar macchi

FISH IN TOMATO & CHILI SAUCE WITH FRIED ONION

This delicious dish, in which firm-fleshed fish is pan-fried until browned and then simmered in an alluringly spiced chili and tomato sauce, originates from northeast India. It is best served with freshly cooked basmati rice and poppadoms.

SERVES: 4

PREP: 10 minutes, plus marinating time

COOK: 35–40 minutes

1½ pounds white fish fillets, such as sole, cod, or halibut, cut into 2-inch pieces

2 tablespoons lemon juice

1 teaspoon salt, or to taste

1 teaspoon ground turmeric

¼ cup vegetable oil or peanut oil, plus extra for pan-frying

2 teaspoons sugar

1 large onion, finely chopped

2 teaspoons ginger paste

2 teaspoons garlic paste

½ teaspoon ground fennel seeds

1 teaspoon ground coriander

½–1 teaspoon chili powder

¾ cup canned diced tomatoes

1¼ cups warm water

2–3 tablespoons chopped fresh cilantro

1 Put the fish onto a large plate and gently rub in the lemon juice, ½ teaspoon of the salt, and ½ teaspoon of the turmeric. Set the fish aside for 15–20 minutes.

2 Pour enough oil into a skillet to fill to a depth of about ½ inch and place over medium–high heat. When the oil is hot, cook the pieces of fish in a single layer until well browned on both sides and a light crust is formed. Drain on paper towels.

3 Heat the ¼ cup of oil in a saucepan or skillet over medium heat and add the sugar. Let it brown, watching it carefully because once it browns it will blacken quickly. As soon as the sugar is brown, add the onion and cook for 5 minutes, until soft. Add the ginger and garlic pastes and cook for an additional 3–4 minutes, or until the mixture begins to brown.

4 Add the ground fennel seeds, ground coriander, chili powder, and the remaining turmeric. Cook for about a minute, then add half the tomatoes. Stir and cook until the tomato juice has evaporated, then add the remaining tomatoes. Continue to cook, stirring, until the oil separates from the spice paste.

5 Pour in the water and add the remaining salt. Bring to a boil and reduce the heat to medium. Add the fish, stir gently, and reduce the heat to low. Cook, uncovered, for 5–6 minutes, then stir in half the chopped cilantro and remove from the heat. Garnish with the remaining cilantro and serve immediately.

Murgh chettinad

PEPPERED SOUTH INDIAN CHICKEN CURRY

This dish originates from Chettinad, which is a region in the state of Tamil Nadu in the most southerly tip of India. Chettinad is well known for its many temples and its delicious cuisine. The latter tends to be on the hot and spicy side, so it is not for the faint-hearted!

SERVES: 4   **PREP:** 25 minutes   **COOK:** 30 minutes

¼ cup vegetable oil or peanut oil

1 teaspoon black mustard seeds

pinch of asafetida or garlic powder

8–10 fresh curry leaves

1¼ pounds skinless, boneless chicken thighs, cut into large bite-size pieces

2 teaspoons ground cumin

1 teaspoon ground coriander

1 teaspoon ground turmeric

2 teaspoons salt

2 tablespoons pepper

1 teaspoon chili powder

1 cup coconut cream or coconut milk

1 cup cold water

1 teaspoon finely grated fresh ginger

juice of 1 lime

⅓ cup finely chopped fresh cilantro

1 Heat the oil in a nonstick saucepan over medium heat. Add the mustard seeds and, when they start to pop, add the asafetida and curry leaves and sauté for 30 seconds.

2 Add the chicken and sauté for 4–5 minutes. Add the cumin, ground coriander, turmeric, salt, pepper, and chili powder and sauté for 1–2 minutes.

3 Add the coconut cream and water, stir to mix well, and cook over low–medium heat for 15–20 minutes, or until the chicken is cooked through and no longer pink in the center.

4 Stir in the ginger, then remove the pan from the heat and stir in the lime juice. Sprinkle with the chopped cilantro and serve immediately.

TIP

Coconut cream is richer and thicker than coconut milk, with more coconut than water. It is available in large supermarkets, in Indian and Asian grocery stores, and online.

Murgh nu farcha

PARSI-STYLE FRIED CHICKEN

In this Parsi-style chicken recipe, chicken pieces are marinated in spices, crumbed, and fried until crisp and golden. For a variation, use turkey breast cutlets instead of the chicken and cut them into finger-thick strips. This dish is delicious served warm.

SERVES: 4

PREP: 15–20 minutes, plus marinating time

COOK: 10–18 minutes

1 teaspoon chili powder

1 fresh green chile, finely chopped

2 teaspoons salt

1 teaspoon ground cumin

1 teaspoon ground coriander

2 teaspoons grated fresh ginger

3 garlic cloves, crushed

1 tablespoon white wine vinegar

1 teaspoon palm sugar or packed light brown sugar

¼ cup finely chopped fresh cilantro

1¼ pounds skinless, boneless chicken breasts, cut into bite-size pieces

3 eggs

1 cup dried white bread crumbs

vegetable oil or peanut oil, for deep-frying

1 Put the chili powder, green chile, salt, cumin, ground coriander, ginger, garlic, vinegar, palm sugar, and chopped cilantro into a mixing bowl. Add the chicken and stir to mix well. Cover and let marinate in the refrigerator for 6–8 hours, or overnight, if possible.

2 Beat the eggs in a shallow bowl. Spread out the bread crumbs on a large plate. Dip the chicken pieces in the beaten egg, then roll in the bread crumbs to coat evenly, shaking off the excess.

3 Heat enough oil for deep-frying in a large saucepan or deep fryer to 350–375°F, or until a cube of bread browns in 30 seconds. Deep-fry the bite-size chicken pieces, in batches, for 5–6 minutes, or until crisp, golden, and cooked all the way through. Remove with a slotted spoon and drain on paper towels. Serve warm.

Tandoori murgh

TANDOORI CHICKEN

This recipe would traditionally be cooked in a tandoor oven—a simple, conical clay oven that is heated by glowing charcoals or wood in its base. For the best flavor, let the chicken marinate for a day before cooking.

SERVES: 4

1 chicken (about 3¼ pounds), skinned
½ lemon
1 teaspoon salt
2 tablespoons ghee or butter, melted
fresh cilantro sprigs, to garnish
lemon wedges, to serve

TANDOORI PASTE

1½ teaspoons garlic paste
1½ teaspoons ginger paste
1 tablespoon ground paprika
1 teaspoon ground cinnamon
1 teaspoon ground cumin
½ teaspoon ground coriander
¼ teaspoon chili powder, ideally Kashmiri chili powder
pinch of ground cloves
¼ teaspoon red food coloring (optional)
a few drops of yellow food coloring (optional)
1 cup plain yogurt

PREP: 5–10 minutes, plus marinating time

1 To make the tandoori paste, combine the garlic and ginger pastes, dry spices, and food coloring (if using) in a bowl and stir in the yogurt. You can use the paste now or store it in an airtight container in the refrigerator for up to 3 days.

2 Use a small knife to make slashes all over the chicken. Rub the lemon half over the chicken, then rub the salt into the slashes. Put the chicken in a deep bowl, add the tandoori paste, and use your hands to rub it all over the chicken and into the slashes. Cover the bowl with plastic wrap and chill in the refrigerator for at least 4 hours, but ideally up to 24 hours.

3 Just before you are ready to cook, preheat the oven to 400°F. Put the chicken on a rack in a roasting pan, breast side up, and drizzle with the melted ghee. Roast in the preheated oven for 45 minutes, then quickly remove the chicken and roasting pan from the oven and turn the temperature to its highest setting.

COOK: 55 minutes–1 hour, plus standing time

4 Carefully pour out any fat from the bottom of the roasting pan. Return the chicken to the oven and roast for an additional 10–15 minutes, until the chicken is tender and the juices run clear when the tip of a sharp knife is inserted into the thickest part of the meat and the paste is lightly charred.

5 Let stand for 10 minutes, then cut into pieces. Garnish with cilantro sprigs and serve with lemon wedges.

Murgh makhani

BUTTER CHICKEN

Before preparing this popular Sikh dish you will need an already-cooked tandoori chicken. Start with the tandoori chicken recipe on the opposite page, or buy roasted chicken—but it won't have as much flavor.

SERVES: 4–6

PREP: 5–10 minutes

COOK: 25 minutes

1 onion, chopped

2 teaspoons garlic paste

2 teaspoons ginger paste

1 (14-ounce) can diced tomatoes

¼–½ teaspoon chili powder

pinch of sugar

pinch of salt

2 tablespoons ghee or vegetable oil or peanut oil

½ cup cold water

1 tablespoon tomato paste

3 tablespoons butter, diced

½ teaspoon garam masala

½ teaspoon ground cumin

½ teaspoon ground coriander

1 cooked tandoori chicken, cut into 8 pieces

¼ cup heavy cream

chopped cashew nuts and fresh cilantro sprigs, to garnish

1 Put the onion, garlic paste, and ginger paste into a food processor or blender and process until a paste forms. Add the tomatoes, chili powder, sugar, and salt and process again until blended.

2 Melt the ghee in a large skillet or wok over medium–high heat. Add the onion-and-tomato mixture and the water and stir in the tomato paste.

3 Bring the mixture to a boil, stirring, then reduce the heat to low and simmer for 5 minutes, stirring occasionally, until the sauce thickens.

4 Stir in half the butter, the garam masala, cumin, and ground coriander. Add the chicken pieces and stir until they are well coated. Simmer for about 10 minutes, or until the chicken is warmed through.

5 Lightly beat the cream in a small bowl and stir in several tablespoons of the hot sauce, beating constantly. Stir the cream mixture into the pan, then add the remaining butter and stir until it melts. Garnish with chopped cashew nuts and cilantro sprigs and serve immediately.

Murgh biryani

CHICKEN BIRYANI

In this dish from the snowy foothills of the Himalayas, the naturally fragrant basmati rice is enhanced with cinnamon, cardamom, and star anise and layered with delicately spiced chicken. It is cooked in a sealed pot to conserve the flavors.

SERVES: 4

⅓ cup plain yogurt

1 tablespoon each garlic paste and ginger paste

1½ pounds skinless, boneless chicken thighs

1 tablespoon white poppy seeds

2 teaspoons coriander seeds

½ mace blade

2 bay leaves, torn into small pieces

½ teaspoon black peppercorns

1 teaspoon cardamom seeds

1-inch piece cinnamon stick

4 cloves

¼ cup ghee or 4 tablespoons butter

1 large onion, finely sliced

1½ teaspoons salt, or to taste

fried onions, to garnish

RICE

pinch of saffron threads, pounded

2 tablespoons hot milk

1½ teaspoons salt

2 (2-inch) cinnamon sticks

3 star anise

2 bay leaves, crumbled

4 cloves

4 green cardamom pods, bruised

2½ cups basmati rice, washed

PREP: 15 minutes, plus marinating & infusing time

1 Put the yogurt and the garlic and ginger pastes into a bowl and beat together with a fork until thoroughly blended. Put the chicken into a nonmetallic bowl, add the yogurt mixture, and mix until well combined. Cover and marinate in the refrigerator for 2 hours.

2 Grind the next eight ingredients (all the seeds and spices) to a fine powder in a spice grinder and set aside.

3 In a flameproof casserole dish large enough to hold the chicken and the rice together, melt the ghee over medium heat, add the onion, and cook, stirring frequently, for 8–10 minutes, until a medium brown.

4 Reduce the heat to low, add the ground seeds and spices, and cook, stirring, for 2–3 minutes. Add the marinated chicken and salt and cook, stirring, for 2 minutes. Turn off the heat and keep the chicken covered.

5 Meanwhile, place the pounded saffron in a small bowl with the hot milk and let steep for 20 minutes.

COOK: 1½ hours, plus standing time

6 Preheat the oven to 350°F. Bring a large saucepan of water to a boil and add the salt and spices. Add the rice, return to a boil, and boil steadily for 2 minutes. Drain the rice, reserving the whole spices, and pile on top of the chicken. Pour the saffron-and-milk mixture over the rice.

7 Soak a piece of wax paper large enough to cover the top of the rice fully and squeeze out the excess water. Lay on top of the rice. Soak a clean dish towel, wring out, and lay loosely on top of the wax paper. Cover the casserole with a piece of aluminum foil. It is important to cover the rice in this way to contain all the steam inside the casserole, because the biryani cooks entirely in the vapor created inside the casserole. Put the lid on top and cook in the center of the preheated oven for 1 hour.

8 Turn off the oven and let the rice stand inside for 30 minutes. Transfer the biryani to serving plates and garnish with the fried onions.

Murgh xacuti

GOAN SPICED CHICKEN

Pronounced "shakutee," this classic, spicy chicken dish from the shores of Goa can be found in almost all the restaurants that dot the beaches, villages, and towns. Made from a blend of coconut milk, red chiles, and aromatic spices, it is best served with some steamed rice and mango chutney.

SERVES: 4　　　**PREP:** 20 minutes　　　**COOK:** 35–40 minutes

6 black peppercorns

3 cloves

2 teaspoons fennel seeds

4 dried red chiles

1 teaspoon cardamom seeds

2 teaspoons white poppy seeds

2 cinnamon sticks

2 teaspoons salt

1 teaspoon ground turmeric

1 teaspoon ground cumin

1 teaspoon ground coriander

¼ cup vegetable oil or peanut oil

1 onion, minced

3 garlic cloves, crushed

1¼ pounds skinless, boneless chicken thighs, cut into bite-size pieces

1¾ cups coconut milk

1¾ cups cold water

1 teaspoon tamarind paste

1 Place a large, nonstick skillet over medium heat and add the peppercorns, cloves, fennel seeds, dried red chiles, cardamom seeds, white poppy seeds, and cinnamon sticks. Dry-fry for 1–2 minutes, then remove from the heat and let cool.

2 Put the cooled whole spices into a spice grinder with the salt, turmeric, cumin and ground coriander. Process until ground to a fairly fine powder.

3 Heat the oil in a large saucepan, add the onion and garlic, and cook over medium heat for 2–3 minutes. Increase the heat to high, add the chicken, and sauté for 5–6 minutes, or until sealed.

4 Add the spice mixture and sauté for 1–2 minutes, then add the coconut milk and water. Bring to a boil, then reduce the heat to low–medium and simmer gently for 15–20 minutes. Stir in the tamarind paste and cook for an additional 2–3 minutes, or until the chicken is cooked all the way through and tender. Serve immediately.

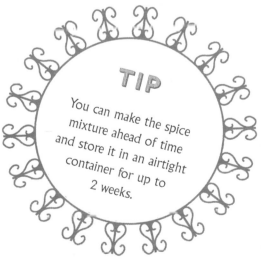

TIP

You can make the spice mixture ahead of time and store it in an airtight container for up to 2 weeks.

Rista

MEATBALLS IN CREAMY CASHEW NUT SAUCE

This delectable recipe comes from Kashmir, the most northerly state in India. This beautiful Himalayan state has a rich culinary heritage—Kashmiri cooking is a work of art and the chefs are extremely skilled as well as creative.

SERVES: 4

PREP: 25–30 minutes, plus soaking & chilling time

COOK: 35–40 minutes

1¼ cups cashew nuts

⅔ cup boiling water

1 pound fresh lean ground lamb

1 tablespoon plain yogurt

1 egg, beaten

½ teaspoon ground cardamom seeds

½ teaspoon freshly ground nutmeg

½ teaspoon pepper

½ teaspoon dried mint

½ teaspoon salt, or to taste

1¼ cups cold water

1-inch piece cinnamon stick

5 green cardamom pods

5 cloves

2 bay leaves

3 tablespoons vegetable oil or peanut oil

1 onion, finely chopped

2 teaspoons garlic paste

1 teaspoon ground ginger

1 teaspoon ground fennel seeds

½ teaspoon ground turmeric

½–1 teaspoon chili powder

⅔ cup heavy cream

1 tablespoon crushed pistachio nuts, to garnish

1 Soak the cashew nuts in a boiling water for 20 minutes.

2 Put the ground lamb into a mixing bowl and add the yogurt, egg, ground cardamom seeds, nutmeg, pepper, mint, and salt. Knead the meat until it is smooth and velvety. Alternatively, put the ingredients into a food processor and process until smooth and combined. Chill the mixture for 30–40 minutes, then divide it into quarters. Make five balls (koftas) out of each quarter, rolling them between your palms to make them smooth and firm.

3 Bring the cold water to a boil in a large, shallow saucepan and add all the whole spices and the bay leaves. Arrange the meatballs in a single layer in the spiced liquid. Reduce the heat to medium, cover the pan, and cook for 12–15 minutes.

4 Remove the meatballs from the pan, cover, and keep hot. Strain the spiced liquid and set aside.

5 Wipe out the pan and add the oil. Place over medium heat and add the onion-and-garlic paste. Cook until the mixture begins to brown and add the ground ginger, ground fennel seeds, turmeric, and chili powder. Sauté for 2–3 minutes, then add the strained liquid and meatballs. Bring to a boil, reduce the heat to low, cover, and simmer for 10–12 minutes.

6 Meanwhile, puree the cashew nuts with their soaking water in a blender and add to the meatball mixture along with the cream. Simmer for an additional 5–6 minutes, then remove from the heat. Garnish with the crushed pistachio nuts and serve immediately.

Keema mattar

SPICED GROUND LAMB WITH PEAS

When the cold winter winds come to northern India, this simple, rustic dish of ground lamb and peas cooked with warming spices makes a popular family meal. Serve with any Indian bread for a filling dinner.

SERVES: 4–6

PREP: 5–10 minutes

COOK: 35–40 minutes

2 tablespoons ghee or vegetable oil or peanut oil

2 teaspoons cumin seeds

1 large onion, finely chopped

1½ teaspoons garlic paste

1½ teaspoons ginger paste

2 bay leaves

1 teaspoon mild, medium, or hot curry powder, to taste

2 tomatoes, seeded and chopped

1 teaspoon ground coriander

¼–½ teaspoon chili powder

¼ teaspoon ground turmeric

pinch of sugar

½ teaspoon salt

½ teaspoon pepper

1 pound fresh lean ground lamb

1⅔ cups frozen peas

1 Melt the ghee in a flameproof casserole dish or large skillet with a tight-fitting lid. Add the cumin seeds and cook, stirring, for 30 seconds, or until they start to crackle.

2 Stir in the onion, garlic and ginger pastes, bay leaves, and curry powder and continue to sauté until the fat separates.

3 Stir in the tomatoes and cook for 1–2 minutes. Add the ground coriander, chili powder, turmeric, sugar, salt, and pepper and stir for 30 seconds.

4 Add the ground lamb and cook, using a wooden spoon to break up the meat, for 5 minutes, or until it is no longer pink. Reduce the heat and simmer, stirring occasionally, for 10 minutes.

5 Add the peas and simmer for an additional 10–15 minutes, until the peas are heated through. If there is too much liquid left in the pan, increase the heat and let it simmer for a few minutes, until it reduces.

Gosht dhansak

SWEET & SOUR LAMB WITH LENTILS

For India's numerous Parsis, this rich dish is served for a Sunday family lunch. The lentils and squash dissolve into a velvety-smooth sauce, and all that is needed to complete the meal are freshly cooked rice and naans.

SERVES: 4

PREP: 20–25 minutes, plus standing time

COOK: 45–50 minutes

1½ pounds boneless shoulder of lamb, trimmed and cut into 2-inch cubes

2 teaspoons salt, or to taste

1½ teaspoons each garlic paste and ginger paste

5 green cardamom pods

1 cup yellow lentils (toor dal)

1 cup chopped butternut or acorn squash

1 carrot, thinly sliced

1 fresh green chile, seeded and chopped

1 teaspoon fenugreek powder

2 cups cold water, plus extra if needed

1 large onion, thinly sliced

2 tablespoons ghee or vegetable oil or peanut oil

2 garlic cloves, crushed

chopped fresh cilantro, to garnish

DHANSAK MASALA

1 teaspoon garam masala

½ teaspoon ground coriander

½ teaspoon ground cumin

½ teaspoon chili powder

½ teaspoon ground turmeric

¼ teaspoon freshly ground cardamom seeds

¼ teaspoon ground cloves

1 Put the lamb and 1 teaspoon of the salt into a large saucepan with enough water to cover and bring to a boil. Reduce the heat and simmer, skimming the surface as necessary until no more foam rises. Stir in the garlic and ginger pastes and cardamom pods and continue simmering for a total of 30 minutes.

2 Meanwhile, put the lentils, squash, carrot, chile, and fenugreek powder into a large, heavy saucepan and pour in the water. Bring to a boil, stirring occasionally, then reduce the heat and simmer for 20–30 minutes, until the lentils and carrot are tender. Stir in a little extra water if the lentils look as though they will catch on the bottom of the pan. Let the lentil mixture cool slightly, then pour it into a food processor or blender and process until a thick, smooth sauce forms.

3 Put the onion in a bowl, sprinkle with the remaining teaspoon of salt, and let stand for about 5 minutes. Use your hands to squeeze out the moisture from the onion.

4 Melt the ghee in a flameproof casserole dish or large skillet with a tight-fitting lid over high heat. Add the onion and cook, stirring constantly, for 2 minutes. Remove one-third of the onion and continue cooking the rest for an additional 1–2 minutes, until golden brown. Use a slotted spoon to immediately remove the onion from the pan; it will continue to darken as it cools. Set aside.

5 Return the one-third of the onion to the pan with the garlic. Stir in all the dhansak masala ingredients and cook for 2 minutes, stirring constantly. Add the cooked lamb and stir for an additional 2 minutes. Add the lentil sauce and simmer over medium heat, stirring and adding a little extra water, if needed, until warmed through. Taste and adjust the seasoning, adding extra salt, if needed. Sprinkle with the reserved onion, garnish with chopped cilantro, and serve immediately.

Kashmiri gosht

KASHMIRI LAMB & FENNEL STEW

This slow-cooked, aromatic lamb stew from Kashmir in northern India almost cooks itself. Kashmiri chili powder is available from Asian grocery stores, but you can make your own by finely grinding dried red Kashmiri chiles in a spice grinder.

SERVES: 4

PREP: 20 minutes

COOK: 2–2¼ hours

¼ cup vegetable oil or peanut oil

2 onions, halved and thinly sliced

1¼ boneless shoulder of lamb, trimmed and cut into bite-size pieces

4 garlic cloves, crushed

2 teaspoons finely grated fresh ginger

1 tablespoon ground coriander

1 teaspoon Kashmiri chili powder

1 teaspoon salt

3 Yukon gold or white round potatoes, halved

2 cups lamb or chicken broth

1 cup light cream

¼ cup ground almonds

2 tablespoons crushed fennel seeds

⅓ cup finely chopped fresh cilantro

2 tablespoons finely chopped fresh mint

1 Heat the oil in a nonstick saucepan and cook the onions over low heat, stirring frequently, for about 15–20 minutes, until lightly browned.

2 Increase the heat to high, add the lamb, and sauté for 4–5 minutes, until sealed. Reduce the heat to medium and add the garlic, ginger, ground coriander, chili powder, and salt. Stir and cook for 1–2 minutes.

3 Add the potatoes and broth, then cover and simmer over low heat for about 1½ hours, or until the lamb is tender.

4 Uncover the pan, increase the heat slightly, and stir in the cream and ground almonds. Cook for an additional 8–10 minutes, until thickened and reduced. Be careful not to boil or the cream will split.

5 Add the crushed fennel seeds to the pan and cook for an additional 3–4 minutes. Remove from the heat and stir in the chopped cilantro and mint. Serve immediately.

TIP

Use a heat diffuser under the pan for even heat distribution when slow-cooking—this prevents the dish from sticking to the bottom and getting burned.

Kolhapuri gosht

KOLHAPURI MUTTON CURRY

This spicy curry originates from the town of Kolhapur in the western state of Maharashtra, which is known for its spicy fare. It is traditionally made with mutton, but you could use lamb. Serve this tasty curry with freshly cooked basmati rice, a cooling cucumber raita, and some tangy lime pickle.

SERVES: 4

PREP: 15–20 minutes, plus cooling time

COOK: 2 hours

3 tablespoons vegetable oil or peanut oil

1¼ pounds boneless shoulder of mutton or lamb, trimmed and cut into bite-size cubes

1 onion, thinly sliced

3 garlic cloves, crushed

1 tablespoon finely grated fresh ginger

1 fresh red chile, finely chopped

1 teaspoon ground turmeric

12 fresh curry leaves

1 (14½-ounce) can diced tomatoes

2 cups lamb or chicken broth

½ cup coconut cream or coconut milk

3 tablespoons finely chopped fresh cilantro, plus extra to garnish

KOLHAPURI MASALA

2 tablespoons coriander seeds

1 tablespoon cumin seeds

1 teaspoon freshly ground cardamom seeds

4 cloves

2 cinnamon sticks

2 dried red chiles

¼ teaspoon freshly grated nutmeg

1 First, make the Kolhapuri masala. Put the coriander seeds, cumin seeds, cardamom seeds, cloves, and cinnamon sticks into a nonstick skillet over low heat. Dry-fry the spices, shaking the pan, for 1 minute, or until fragrant. Remove from the heat and let cool, then put into a spice grinder with the dried red chile and nutmeg. Grind to a powder and set aside.

2 Heat 1 tablespoon of the oil in a heavy saucepan over medium–high heat. Brown the meat, in batches, for 3–4 minutes. Remove the meat from the pan with a slotted spoon and set aside.

3 Add the remaining oil to the pan and reduce the heat to medium. Cook the onion, stirring, for 2–3 minutes, until softened. Add the garlic, ginger, fresh red chile, turmeric, and curry leaves and cook for 1 minute, until fragrant.

4 Add the Kolhapuri masala and stir well to combine, then return the meat to the pan, stirring to coat in the onion mixture. Add the chopped tomatoes and broth and bring to a boil. Reduce the heat to low and simmer, uncovered, for 1½ hours, or until the meat is tender.

5 Stir in the coconut cream and chopped cilantro, then cook for an additional 10 minutes, or until the sauce has thickened. Garnish with extra chopped cilantro and serve immediately.

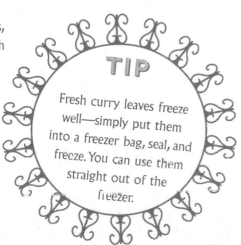

TIP

Fresh curry leaves freeze well—simply put them into a freezer bag, seal, and freeze. You can use them straight out of the freezer.

Vindaloo

PORK WITH CHILES, VINEGAR & GARLIC

The name *vindaloo* is derived from two Portuguese words—*vin*, meaning "vinegar," and *alho*, meaning "garlic." When the Portuguese traveled to India, they took pork preserved in vinegar, garlic, and pepper, which was spiced up to suit Indian tastes and this dish was born.

SERVES: 4

PREP: 15–20 minutes, plus marinating time

COOK: 1¼–1½ hours

2–6 dried red chiles, torn

5 whole cloves

1-inch piece cinnamon stick, broken up

4 green cardamom pods

½ teaspoon black peppercorns

½ mace blade

¼ nutmeg, lightly crushed

1 teaspoon cumin seeds

1½ teaspoons coriander seeds

½ teaspoon fenugreek seeds

2 teaspoons garlic paste

1 tablespoon ginger paste

3 tablespoons apple cider vinegar or white wine vinegar

1 tablespoon tamarind juice or juice of ½ lime

1½ pounds boneless leg of pork, cut into 1-inch cubes

¼ cup vegetable oil or peanut oil, plus 2 teaspoons

2 large onions, finely chopped

1¼ cups warm water

1 teaspoon salt, or to taste

1 teaspoon packed dark brown sugar

2 large garlic cloves, finely sliced

8–10 fresh curry leaves

1 Grind the first ten ingredients (all the spices) to a fine powder in a spice grinder. Transfer the ground spices to a bowl and add the garlic and ginger pastes, vinegar, and tamarind juice. Mix together to form a paste.

2 Put the pork into a large, nonmetallic bowl and rub about one-quarter of the spice paste into the meat. Cover and let marinate in the refrigerator for 30–40 minutes.

3 Heat the oil in a heavy saucepan over medium heat, add the onions, and cook, stirring frequently, for 8–10 minutes, until lightly browned. Add the remaining spice paste and cook, stirring constantly, for 5–6 minutes.
Add 2 tablespoons of the water and cook until it evaporates. Repeat with another 2 tablespoons of water.

4 Add the marinated pork and cook over medium–high heat for 5–6 minutes. Add the salt, sugar, and the remaining water. Bring to a boil, then reduce the heat to low, cover, and simmer for 50–55 minutes.

5 Meanwhile, heat the 2 teaspoons of oil in a small saucepan over low heat. Add the sliced garlic and cook, stirring, until it begins to brown. Add the curry leaves and let sizzle for 15–20 seconds. Stir the garlic mixture into the pan. Serve immediately.

CHAPTER 4
LEGUMES

Rasam

SOUTH INDIAN LENTIL BROTH

Rice is a staple dish in south India and is served at almost every meal. It is usually accompanied by this spiced lentil broth and served with *pachadis* (south Indian raitas) and dry curried vegetables. *Rasam* is a thin liquid preparation that can also be eaten as a soup.

SERVES: 4

PREP: 10 minutes

COOK: 30–35 minutes

½ cup pigeon peas (tuvaar dal) or black-eyed peas

2½ cups cold water

1 teaspoon ground turmeric

2 tablespoons vegetable oil or peanut oil

1 teaspoon black mustard seeds

6–8 fresh curry leaves

1 teaspoon cumin seeds

1 fresh green chile

1 teaspoon tamarind paste

1 teaspoon salt

1 Rinse the pigeon peas under cold running water. Put the pigeon peas into a saucepan with the water, turmeric, and 1 tablespoon of the oil. Cover and simmer for 25–30 minutes, or until the lentils are cooked and tender.

2 Heat the remaining oil in a skillet over medium heat. Add the mustard seeds, curry leaves, cumin seeds, chile, and tamarind paste. When the seeds start to pop, remove the pan from the heat and add to the lentil mixture with the salt.

3 Return the broth to the heat for 2–3 minutes. Ladle into small serving bowls and serve immediately with steamed basmati rice.

Tarka dal
LENTILS WITH CUMIN & SHALLOTS

This dish, traditionally known as *tarka dal,* is easy to cook. The word *tarka* means "tempering"—a boiled dal is tempered with a few whole spices, and chopped shallots are added to the hot oil before being folded into the cooked lentils.

SERVES: 4

PREP: 10–15 minutes

COOK: 1 hour

1 cup split red lentils (masoor dal)

3½ cups cold water

1 teaspoon salt, or to taste

2 teaspoons vegetable oil or peanut oil

½ teaspoon black or brown mustard seeds

½ teaspoon cumin seeds

4 shallots, finely chopped

2 fresh green chiles, chopped (seeded, if desired)

1 teaspoon ground turmeric

1 teaspoon ground cumin

1 fresh tomato, chopped

2 tablespoons chopped fresh cilantro

1 Put the lentils into a strainer and rinse under cold running water. Drain and put into a saucepan. Add the water and bring to a boil. Reduce the heat to medium and skim the surface to remove the foam. Cook, uncovered, for 10 minutes. Reduce the heat to low, cover, and cook, stirring occasionally to make sure that the lentils do not stick to the bottom of the pan as they thicken, for 45 minutes. Stir in the salt.

2 Meanwhile, heat the oil in a small saucepan over medium heat. When hot but not smoking, add the mustard seeds, followed by the cumin seeds. Add the shallots and chiles and cook, stirring, for 2–3 minutes, then add the turmeric and ground cumin. Add the tomato and cook, stirring, for 30 seconds.

3 Fold the shallot mixture into the cooked lentils. Stir in the chopped cilantro, remove from the heat, and serve immediately.

Moong dal khichdee

YELLOW SPLIT MUNG BEAN & RICE PILAF

This classic Gujarati rice and lentil preparation is a warming and comforting dish, particularly if someone is feeling under the weather. It is delicious served with a dollop of plain yogurt, green chile pickle (see page 50), and your favorite chutney. Split yellow mung beans are widely available and do not require soaking.

SERVES: 4

PREP: 10 minutes

COOK: 20–25 minutes, plus standing time

1 cup split yellow mung beans (moong dal)

1 cup basmati rice

2 tablespoons ghee or vegetable oil or peanut oil

6–8 black peppercorns

2 teaspoons cumin seeds

4 garlic cloves, finely chopped

2 teaspoons salt

¼ teaspoon ground turmeric

4¼ cups boiling water

1 Put the mung beans and rice into a strainer and rinse under cold running water. Drain and set aside.

2 Heat the ghee in a heavy saucepan over medium heat. Add the reserved mung bean-and-rice mixture and sauté gently for 1–2 minutes.

3 Add the peppercorns, cumin seeds, garlic, salt, and turmeric and sauté for 1–2 minutes. Pour in the water.

4 Bring to a boil, then cover tightly and reduce the heat to low. Cook, without stirring, for 12–15 minutes, then remove from the heat (without lifting the lid) and let stand for 12–15 minutes.

5 To serve, remove the lid and gently fluff up the grains with a fork. Serve immediately.

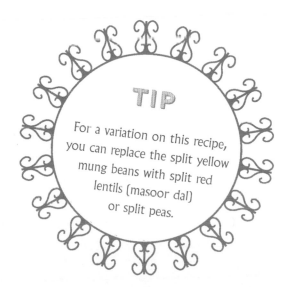

TIP

For a variation on this recipe, you can replace the split yellow mung beans with split red lentils (masoor dal) or split peas.

Ma ki dal

SPICED BLACK LENTILS

Using whole black lentils with their skins still on, instead of split lentils or beans, adds a gelatinous texture to this rich dish. It is time-consuming so is usually prepared for a special occasion rather than on an everyday basis.

SERVES: 4–6

PREP: 10–15 minutes, plus soaking time

COOK: 3½ hours

1¼ cups whole black lentils (urad dal sabat)

⅔ cup dried red kidney beans

4 garlic cloves, cut in half

4 black cardamom pods, lightly crushed

2 bay leaves

1 cinnamon stick

1 stick butter

¾ teaspoon garlic paste

¾ teaspoon ginger paste

2 tablespoons tomato paste

½ teaspoon chili powder

pinch of sugar

⅔ cup heavy cream

salt, to taste

fresh cilantro sprigs, to garnish

1 Put the lentils and kidney beans into separate bowls with plenty of water to cover and let soak for at least 3 hours, but preferably overnight.

2 Meanwhile, put the garlic cloves, cardamom pods, bay leaves, and cinnamon stick into a piece of cheesecloth and tie together into a bundle.

3 Drain the lentils and kidney beans separately. Put the kidney beans into a large saucepan with twice their volume of water and bring to a boil, then boil for 10 minutes. Drain well.

4 Return the kidney beans to the pan, add the black lentils, and cover with double their volume of water. Add the spice bag and bring to a boil over high heat. Reduce the heat to low, partly cover the pan, and simmer, skimming the surface as necessary to remove the foam, for about 3 hours, until the legumes are tender and reduced to a thick paste. Mash the lentils and beans against the side of the pan with a wooden spoon every 15 minutes while they are simmering and stir in extra water if it evaporates before the legumes are tender.

5 When the lentils and beans are almost cooked, remove the spice bag and set aside to cool.

6 Melt the butter into a small saucepan. Add the garlic and ginger pastes and stir around for 1 minute. Stir in the tomato paste, chili powder, sugar, and salt and continue simmering for 2–3 minutes.

7 When the spice bag is cool enough to handle, squeeze all the flavoring juices into the lentils and beans. Stir the butter-and-spice mixture into the legumes, along with all but 2 tablespoons of the cream. Bring the mixture to a boil, then reduce the heat and simmer, stirring occasionally, for 10 minutes.

8 Transfer the dal to a serving dish, then swirl the remaining cream over the top and garnish with cilantro sprigs.

Khichdee
KITCHRI

This recipe makes a light meal on its own, served with Indian bread and a raita, but it is also excellent to team with other vegetarian dishes. This is the traditional Indian dish that British cooks of the Raj adapted into kedgeree.

SERVES: 4–6

1¼ cups basmati rice

1¼ cups split red lentils (masoor dal)

2 tablespoons ghee or vegetable oil or peanut oil

1 large onion, finely chopped

2 teaspoons garam masala

1½ teaspoons salt, or to taste

pinch of asafetida or garlic powder

3½ cups cold water

2 tablespoons chopped fresh cilantro

PREP: 5–10 minutes, plus soaking time

1 Rinse the rice in several changes of water until the water runs clear, then let soak for 30 minutes. Drain and set aside until ready to cook.

2 Meanwhile, put the lentils into a strainer and rinse under cold running water. Drain and set aside.

3 Melt the ghee in a flameproof casserole dish or a large saucepan over medium–high heat. Add the onion and sauté for 5–8 minutes, until golden but not brown.

4 Add the reserved rice and lentils along with the garam masala, salt, and asafetida, and stir for 2 minutes. Pour in the water and bring to a boil, stirring.

COOK: 35–40 minutes, plus standing time

5 Reduce the heat to the lowest setting and cover the pan tightly. Simmer, without lifting the lid, for 20 minutes, until the grains are tender and the liquid is absorbed. With the pan covered, turn off the heat and let stand for 5 minutes.

6 Use a fork to fluff up the grains of rice. Mix in the chopped cilantro and adjust the seasoning, adding extra salt, if needed. Serve immediately.

Cholar dal

SPICED BENGAL GRAM

Traditionally eaten during religious celebrations, this spiced dal from Bengal is delicious with pooris or rice.

The lentils used in this preparation are commonly known as split yellow lentils or *chana dal*, but they are

sometimes referred to as Bengal gram. They do not need overnight soaking before cooking.

SERVES: 4

PREP: 15 minutes

COOK: 40–45 minutes

1¼ cups split yellow lentils (chana dal)

3½ cups cold water, plus extra if needed

⅓ cup ghee or 5 tablespoons butter

1 small onion, minced

2 fresh green chiles, slit lengthwise

1 tablespoon ground coriander

1 teaspoon ground cumin

2 bay leaves

1 teaspoon hot chili powder

1 teaspoon ground turmeric

2 dried red chiles

2 garlic cloves, finely sliced

2 teaspoon grated fresh ginger

1 tablespoon raisins

2 teaspoon salt

2 tablespoons lightly toasted, dry unsweetened coconut, to garnish

1 Put the lentils into a strainer and rinse under cold running water. Drain.

2 Put the lentils and water into a saucepan, stir well, and bring to a boil, skimming the surface as necessary to remove the foam. Reduce the heat, cover, and simmer, stirring frequently and adding more water, if needed, for 35–40 minutes, or until the lentils are just tender.

3 Remove the pan from the heat and beat to break down the lentils. Set aside and keep warm.

4 Meanwhile, heat the ghee in a nonstick skillet over medium heat. Add the onion and sauté for 4–5 minutes.

5 Add the fresh green chiles, ground coriander, cumin, bay leaves, chili powder, turmeric, dried red chiles, garlic, and ginger and sauté for 1–2 minutes. Add the raisins, stir, and cook for 30 seconds.

6 Remove from the heat and pour the spice mixture over the lentils. Stir in the salt, mix well, and heat through. Garnish with the toasted coconut and serve immediately.

Khatti meethi dal

SWEET & SOUR LENTILS

Indian cooks never seem to run out of ideas for making something special out of simple, inexpensive ingredients. This is another Bengali style of preparing split yellow lentils with sweet flavors from the coconut and sugar along with sour flavors from the asafetida and tamarind.

SERVES: 4

PREP: 5–10 minutes

COOK: 1 hour

1¼ cups split yellow lentils (chana dal)

5 cups cold water

2 bay leaves, torn

3 fresh green chiles, slit lengthwise

½ teaspoon ground turmeric

½ teaspoon asafetida or garlic powder

3 tablespoons vegetable oil or peanut oil

½ onion, finely chopped

¾-inch piece fresh ginger, finely chopped

⅓ cup grated coconut

1 fresh green chile, chopped (seeded, if desired)

1½ tablespoons sugar, or to taste

1½ tablespoons tamarind paste, or to taste

½ teaspoon garam masala

¼ teaspoon ground cumin

¼ teaspoon ground coriander

salt, to taste

GARNISH

1 tablespoon ghee or butter, melted

1 teaspoon garam masala

2 tablespoons chopped fresh cilantro

1 Put the lentils into a strainer and rinse under cold running water. Drain and put into a large saucepan with the water. Place over high heat and bring to a boil, skimming the surface as necessary to remove the foam. When the foam stops rising, stir in the bay leaves, whole green chiles, turmeric, and asafetida. Partly cover the pan and continue to simmer for about 40 minutes, or until the lentils are tender and the liquid has been absorbed.

2 Meanwhile, heat the oil in a large skillet over medium–high heat. Add the onion and ginger and sauté for 5–8 minutes. Stir in the coconut, chopped green chile, sugar, tamarind paste, garam masala, cumin, and ground coriander and stir for about 1 minute.

3 Add the cooked lentils to the spice mixture and stir well to combine. Taste and adjust the seasoning, adding salt and extra sugar and tamarind, if needed.

4 Transfer the lentils to a serving dish and drizzle the melted ghee over the top. Sprinkle with the garam masala and chopped cilantro and serve immediately.

TIP

Never add salt to lentils before they are cooked and tender. Salt will draw out any moisture, so the lentils will remain too dehydrated to digest easily.

Masala dal

MIXED LENTILS WITH FIVE-SPICE SEASONING

Bengali five-spice seasoning, or *panch phoran*, is a typical combination of spices used in eastern and north-eastern India. Here, the whole spices are fried briefly in hot oil to release their fragrant aromas and added to the cooked lentils to "temper" them.

SERVES: 4–6

PREP: 5–10 minutes

COOK: 30–35 minutes

⅔ cup split red lentils (masoor dal)

⅔ cup split yellow mung beans (moong dal)

3½ cups hot water, plus extra if needed

1 teaspoon ground turmeric

1 teaspoon salt

1 tablespoon lemon juice

2 tablespoons vegetable oil or peanut oil

¼ teaspoon black mustard seeds

¼ teaspoon cumin seeds

¼ teaspoon nigella seeds

¼ teaspoon fennel seeds

4–5 fenugreek seeds

2–3 dried red chiles

GARNISH

1 small tomato, seeded and cut into strips

fresh cilantro sprigs

1 Put the lentils and mung beans into a strainer and rinse under cold running water. Drain and put them into a saucepan with the water. Bring to a boil, then reduce the heat slightly and boil for 5–6 minutes, skimming the surface as necessary to remove the foam. When the foam stops rising, add the turmeric, reduce the heat to low, cover, and cook for 20 minutes. Add the salt and lemon juice and beat the dal to break up the legumes. Add a little more water if the dal is too thick.

2 Heat the oil in a small saucepan over medium heat. When hot but not smoking, add the mustard seeds. As soon as they begin to pop, reduce the heat to low and add the cumin seeds, nigella seeds, fennel seeds, fenugreek seeds, and dried chiles. Let the spices sizzle until the seeds begin to pop and the chiles have blackened. Remove from the heat immediately.

3 Transfer the cooked lentils and beans to a serving dish. Pour over the spice mixture, scraping off every bit from the pan. Garnish with the tomato strips and cilantro sprigs and serve immediately.

Vatana gashi

CHICKPEAS IN COCONUT MILK

This simple but delicious dish hails from the palm-fringed southern coast of India, where coconut milk is used as an everyday broth. Traditionally, dried chickpeas would be used, but canned ones are a time-saving alternative.

SERVES: 4

PREP: 5–10 minutes

COOK: 15–20 minutes

2 Yukon gold or white round potatoes, cut into ½-inch cubes

1 cup hot water

1 (15-ounce) can chickpeas, drained and rinsed

1 cup coconut milk

1 teaspoon salt

2 tablespoons vegetable oil or peanut oil

4 large garlic cloves, finely chopped or crushed

2 teaspoons ground coriander

½ teaspoon ground turmeric

½–1 teaspoon chili powder

juice of ½ lemon

1 Put the potatoes into a saucepan and add the water. Bring to a boil, then reduce the heat to low and cook, covered, for 6–7 minutes, until the potatoes are almost cooked through. Add the chickpeas and cook, uncovered, for 3–4 minutes, until the potatoes are tender. Add the coconut milk and salt and bring to a slow simmer.

2 Meanwhile, heat the oil in a small saucepan over low heat. Add the garlic and cook, stirring frequently, until it begins to brown. Add the ground coriander, turmeric, and chili powder and cook, stirring, for 25–30 seconds.

3 Fold the spiced oil into the chickpea mixture. Stir in the lemon juice and remove from the heat. Serve immediately.

TIP

You can use green beans or a mixture of green beans and carrots instead of the potatoes. Black-eyed peas are also excellent for this recipe.

Chhole tamattar

CHICKPEAS WITH SPICED TOMATOES

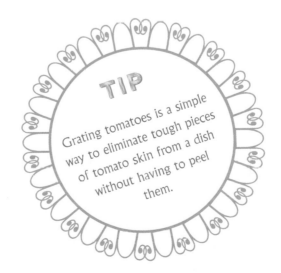

In the Punjab, chickpeas are popular all year round and are often included in Sikh festive meals. Here, they are made into a versatile salad that can be enjoyed as part of a vegetarian meal.

SERVES: 4

PREP: 10–15 minutes

COOK: 25–30 minutes

⅓ cup vegetable oil or peanut oil

2 teaspoons cumin seeds

3 large onions, finely chopped

1 teaspoon garlic paste

1 teaspoon ginger paste

2 small fresh green chiles, seeded and thinly sliced

1½ teaspoons dried mango powder (amchoor)

1½ teaspoons garam masala

¾ teaspoon asafetida or garlic powder

½ teaspoon ground turmeric

¼–1 teaspoon chili powder

3 large, firm tomatoes (about 1 pound), grated

1 (29-ounce) can chickpeas, drained and rinsed

⅓ cup water

1 bunch fresh spinach (about 10 ounces), tough stems removed

½ teaspoon salt, or to taste

1 Heat the oil in a large skillet over medium–high heat. Add the cumin seeds and stir around for 30 seconds, or until they brown and crackle, watching carefully because they can burn quickly.

2 Add the onions, garlic and ginger pastes, and chiles and sauté for 5–8 minutes, until the onions are golden.

3 Stir in the dried mango powder, garam masala, asafetida, turmeric, and chili powder. Add the tomatoes to the pan and continue to cook, stirring frequently, until the sauce blends together and starts to brown slightly.

4 Stir in the chickpeas and water and bring to a boil. Reduce the heat to low and use a wooden spoon or a potato masher to mash about one-quarter of the chickpeas, leaving the remainder whole.

5 Add the spinach to the pan and stir until it begins to wilt. Stir in the salt, then taste and adjust the seasoning, adding extra salt, if needed. Serve immediately.

TIP

Grating tomatoes is a simple way to eliminate tough pieces of tomato skin from a dish without having to peel them.

Chaat

CHICKPEAS WITH POTATO & SPICED YOGURT

This sweet yet savory and slightly spicy dish can be found all over India. The base is a store-bought, crispy-fried puffed "cracker" called *panipuri*, which is available from Asian grocery stores. If you cannot get hold of them, you can use any thin, wheat crackers you can find. *Sev* are thin, crispy strands of spiced, fried chickpea flour.

SERVES: 4

PREP: 20 minutes, plus soaking time

COOK: 25–30 minutes

1 cup dried chickpeas

1¾ cups plain yogurt

1 teaspoon grated fresh ginger

1 teaspoon chili powder

½ teaspoon ground cumin

½ teaspoon ground coriander

1 teaspoon salt

¼ teaspoon pepper

32 panipuris or thin, wheat crackers

2 large russet or Yukon gold potatoes, peeled, boiled, and coarsely mashed

⅓ cup sweet chili sauce

⅓ cup cilantro chutney (see page 40)

1 small red onion, very finely diced

¼ cup finely chopped fresh cilantro

¼ cup sev

2 tablespoons pomegranate seeds

1 Soak the chickpeas in a bowl of cold water for 6–8 hours, or overnight. Drain, then put the chickpeas into a saucepan of cold water and bring to a boil. Cook for 25–30 minutes, or until tender. Drain well and set aside

2 Whisk the yogurt in a bowl until smooth, then stir in the ginger, chili powder, ground cumin, ground coriander, salt, and pepper. Set aside.

3 Break each panipuri gently with a fork to create a tiny opening on the top. Arrange the panipuris in a single layer on a large serving plate.

4 Place a spoonful of the potato on top of each panipuri. Divide the chickpeas among the panipuri and drizzle with the spiced yogurt. Spoon the sweet chili sauce and cilantro chutney on top. Sprinkle with the red onion, chopped cilantro, and sev. Finally, sprinkle with the pomegranate seeds and serve immediately.

TIP

You can prepare the chickpeas and spiced yogurt for this dish in advance, but the rest must be assembled just before serving.

Rajma

RED KIDNEY BEAN CURRY

High in fiber, this delicious northern Indian dish of spiced red kidney beans is best served with rice and warm flatbreads. It can easily be made a day ahead—prepare it up to the end of step 3. When you are ready to serve, simply warm it through and add the yogurt and chopped cilantro.

SERVES: 4

PREP: 20 minutes

COOK: 30–35 minutes

2 tablespoons vegetable oil or peanut oil

2 teaspoons cumin seeds

2 onions, finely chopped

2 teaspoons grated fresh ginger

6 garlic cloves, crushed

2 fresh green chiles, finely chopped

2 large tomatoes, coarsely chopped

2 teaspoons ground coriander

1 teaspoon ground cumin

¼ teaspoon ground turmeric

1 teaspoon garam masala

1 (28-ounce) can red kidney beans, drained and rinsed

1 teaspoon palm sugar or packed light brown sugar

2 cups warm water

1 teaspoon salt

¼ cup finely chopped fresh cilantro, to garnish

plain yogurt, to serve

1 Heat the oil in a large saucepan and add the cumin seeds. When they stop crackling, add the onions and sauté until they are soft.

2 Add the ginger and garlic and sauté for 2 minutes. Add the green chiles, tomatoes, ground coriander, cumin, turmeric, and garam masala and sauté for 12–15 minutes.

3 Add the red kidney beans, palm sugar, water, and salt and cook for 10–12 minutes, or until the beans are soft.

4 Remove from the heat and transfer to a serving dish. Garnish with the chopped cilantro and serve with a spoonful of yogurt.

TIP

Canned beans are used in this recipe for speed. If using dried beans, cook according to the package directions before using.

CHAPTER 5
RICE & BREADS

Pulao

PILAU RICE

Colorful pilau rice is the perfect accompaniment to a whole range of Indian dishes. For the authentic flavor and texture, it is important to use basmati rice instead of any other long-grain rice. Don't be tempted to omit the soaking stage.

SERVES: 2–4

1 cup basmati rice
2 tablespoons ghee or butter
3 green cardamom pods
2 cloves
3 black peppercorns
½ teaspoon salt
½ teaspoon saffron threads
1¾ cups cold water

PREP: 5 minutes, plus soaking time

1 Wash the rice in several changes of water until the water runs clear, then let soak in a bowl of fresh cold water for 30 minutes. Drain and set aside.

2 Melt the ghee in a heavy saucepan over medium–high heat. Add the cardamom pods, cloves, and peppercorns and sauté for 1 minute. Add the rice and sauté for an additional 2 minutes.

COOK: 25–30 minutes

3 Add the salt, saffron, and water to the rice mixture. Bring to a boil, then reduce the heat to low, cover, and simmer for 20 minutes, or according to the package directions, until all the water has been absorbed.

4 Use a fork to fluff up the grains of rice. Transfer to a large serving dish and serve hot.

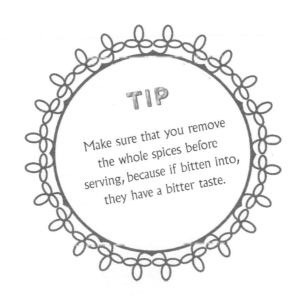

TIP

Make sure that you remove the whole spices before serving, because if bitten into, they have a bitter taste.

Dahi bhaat

SPICED RICE WITH YOGURT & CUCUMBER

This delightful dish from southern India consists of rice combined with a seasoned yogurt-and-cucumber mixture and finished off with a tempered spiced oil (also known as *tarka*). Serve on its own or with curried vegetables and a fresh relish.

SERVES: 4

PREP: 25 minutes

COOK: 15 minutes, plus standing time

1⅔ cups basmati rice

4 tablespoons ghee or butter

2 teaspoons salt

2½ cups boiling water

2 fresh green chiles, split lengthwise and seeded

1 tablespoon finely chopped fresh ginger

¼ cup cold water

1¾ cups plain yogurt, whisked

⅓ cup finely chopped fresh cilantro

1 teaspoon sugar

½ cucumber, finely diced

1 teaspoon white lentils (urad dal, optional)

2 teaspoons black mustard seeds

2 teaspoons cumin seeds

2 dried red chiles

6–8 fresh curry leaves

2 garlic cloves, thinly sliced

1 Put the rice into a heavy saucepan with 1 tablespoon of the ghee and 1 teaspoon of the salt and add the boiling water. Bring to a boil, then reduce the heat to low, cover tightly, and simmer for 10–12 minutes. Remove from the heat and let stand, without lifting the lid, for 12–15 minutes.

2 Meanwhile, in a spice grinder or small food processor, process the chiles and ginger with the cold water until smooth.

3 Put the yogurt into a large bowl and add the chile mixture along with the chopped cilantro, sugar, cucumber, and remaining salt. Mix well.

4 When the rice has finished standing, uncover and fluff up the grains with a fork. Transfer to a serving dish, spoon the yogurt mixture over the rice, and toss to mix well.

5 Melt the remaining ghee in a skillet. When hot, add the white lentils, if using, and the mustard seeds and cumin seeds. As soon as they start to pop, add the dried red chiles, curry leaves, and garlic. Sauté for 30–40 seconds, then remove from the heat and pour the spiced oil over the rice mixture. Toss to mix well. Serve warm.

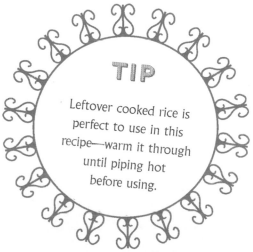

TIP

Leftover cooked rice is perfect to use in this recipe—warm it through until piping hot before using.

Nimbu chawal

LEMON-LACED BASMATI RICE

In this appetizing rice dish, the grains of basmati rice are tinged with yellow turmeric and adorned with black mustard seeds. The main flavor here is that of curry leaves, which is the hallmark of south Indian cuisine.

SERVES: 4

1¼ cups basmati rice

2 tablespoons vegetable oil or peanut oil

½ teaspoon black or brown mustard seeds

10–12 fresh curry leaves

¼ cup cashew nuts

¼ teaspoon ground turmeric

1 teaspoon salt

2 cups hot water

2 tablespoons lemon juice

1 tablespoon snipped fresh chives, to garnish

PREP: 5 minutes, plus soaking time

1 Wash the rice in several changes of water until the water runs clear, then let soak in a bowl of fresh cold water for 20 minutes. Drain and set aside.

2 Heat the oil in a nonstick saucepan over medium heat. When hot but not smoking, add the mustard seeds, followed by the curry leaves and the cashew nuts (in that order).

3 Stir in the turmeric, quickly followed by the reserved rice and the salt. Cook, stirring, for 1 minute, then add the hot water and lemon juice. Stir once, bring to a boil, and boil for 2 minutes.

COOK: 12 minutes, plus standing time

4 Cover tightly, reduce the heat to low, and cook for 8 minutes. Turn off the heat and let stand, without lifting the lid, for 6–7 minutes.

5 Use a fork to fluff up the grains of rice. Transfer to a serving dish, garnish with the chives and serve immediately.

Chaunke hue chawal

SPICED BASMATI RICE

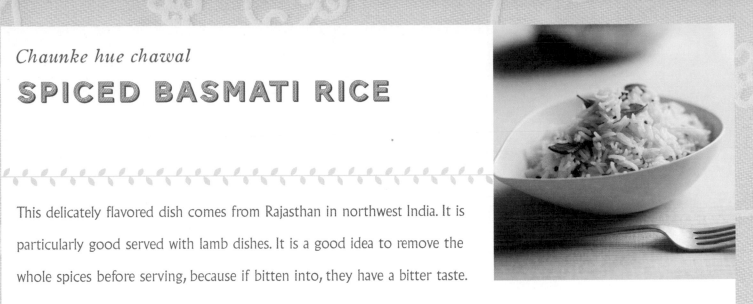

This delicately flavored dish comes from Rajasthan in northwest India. It is particularly good served with lamb dishes. It is a good idea to remove the whole spices before serving, because if bitten into, they have a bitter taste.

SERVES: 4–6

1¼ cups basmati rice

2 tablespoons ghee or vegetable oil or peanut oil

5 green cardamom pods, bruised

5 cloves

½ cinnamon stick

1 teaspoon fennel seeds

½ teaspoon black mustard seeds

2 bay leaves

2 cups cold water

1½ teaspoons salt, or to taste

pepper, to taste

PREP: 5 minutes, plus soaking time

1 Wash the rice in several changes of water until the water runs clear, then let soak in a bowl of fresh cold water for 30 minutes. Drain and set aside.

2 Melt the ghee in a large saucepan over medium–high heat. Add the spices and bay leaves and stir for 30 seconds. Stir the reserved rice into the pan so the grains are coated with ghee.

3 Stir in the water and salt and bring to a boil. Reduce the heat to the lowest setting and cover the pan tightly. Simmer, without lifting the lid, for 8–10 minutes, until the grains are tender and all the liquid is absorbed.

COOK: 10–12 minutes, plus standing time

4 Turn off the heat and use a fork to fluff up the grains of rice. Adjust the seasoning, adding extra salt and pepper, if needed. Replace the lid and let stand for 5 minutes before serving.

TIP

For spiced saffron rice, bring the water to a boil and stir in 1 teaspoon of saffron threads. Let steep while the rice soaks, then add to the pan in step 3.

Vangi bhaat

EGGPLANT & TOMATO RICE

This one-dish rice meal from Maharashtra is equally good when eaten on its own with a big spoonful of yogurt and a crisp poppadam, or as a delicious accompaniment to curries. Variations of this dish can be found throughout southern India, especially in the states of Andhra Pradesh and Karnataka.

SERVES: 4

PREP: 25 minutes, plus soaking time

COOK: 20–25 minutes, plus standing time

1½ cups basmati rice

¼ cup vegetable oil or peanut oil

2 tablespoons ghee or butter

4 shallots, finely chopped

2 garlic cloves, finely chopped

1 cinnamon stick

4 green cardamom pods

3 cloves

2 teaspoons cumin seeds

1 eggplant, trimmed and cut into ½-inch dice

4 ripe tomatoes, skinned, seeded, and finely chopped

2 teaspoons salt

1 teaspoon pepper

2½ cups boiling water

⅓ cup finely chopped fresh cilantro

1 Wash the rice in several changes of water until the water runs clear, then let soak in a bowl of fresh cold water for 20 minutes. Drain and set aside.

2 Heat the oil and ghee in a heavy saucepan over medium heat. Sauté the shallots, garlic, cinnamon stick, cardamom pods, cloves, and cumin seeds for 4–5 minutes, until soft and fragrant.

3 Add the eggplant and sauté over medium heat for 4–5 minutes. Add the tomatoes and the reserved rice and stir to mix well. Add the salt and pepper and pour in the water. Bring to a boil, then cover the pan tightly, reduce the heat to low, and cook for 10–12 minutes. Remove from the heat and let stand, without lifting the lid, for 10 minutes.

4 When ready to serve, uncover and use a fork to fluff up the grains of rice. Stir in the chopped cilantro and serve immediately.

Thengai sadam

COCONUT RICE

Thanks to the abundance of coconut palms in the southern coastal regions of India, coconut—in its various guises—is a common ingredient in southern Indian cuisine. However, it also plays an essential role in religious ceremonies throughout India and South Asia. Fittingly, this dish is ideal for special occasions.

SERVES: 4–6

1¼ cups basmati rice

2 tablespoons peanut oil combined with 1 teaspoon dry mustard

2 cups coconut milk

1½ teaspoons salt, or to taste

PREP: 5–10 minutes, plus soaking time

1 Wash the rice in several changes of water until the water runs clear, then let soak in a bowl of fresh cold water for 30 minutes. Drain and set aside.

2 When you are ready to cook, heat the peanut oil and dry mustard over medium–high heat. Add the reserved rice and stir until the grains are coated in oil. Add the coconut milk and bring to a boil.

COOK: 15–20 minutes, plus standing time

3 Reduce the heat to its lowest setting, stir in the salt, and cover the pan tightly. Simmer, without lifting the lid, for 8–10 minutes, until the rice is tender and all the liquid has been absorbed.

4 Turn off the heat and use a fork to fluff up the grains of rice. Taste and adjust the seasoning, adding extra salt, if needed. Replace the lid on the pan and let the rice stand for 5 minutes before serving.

Mirch-dhaniye ke naan

CHILE-CILANTRO NAAN

Naan is a type of leavened flatbread that came to India with the ancient Persians—it means "bread" in their language. Naan is traditionally made by slapping the rolled and shaped dough against the hot inside of a charcoal-heated tandoor oven, but it can also be cooked under a hot broiler.

MAKES: 8

PREP: 20–25 minutes, plus resting time

COOK: 30–35 minutes

3⅔ cups all-purpose flour

2 teaspoons sugar

1 teaspoon salt

1 teaspoon baking powder

1 egg

1 cup milk

2 tablespoons vegetable oil or peanut oil, plus extra for brushing

2 fresh red chiles, chopped (seeded, if preferred)

⅓ cup chopped fresh cilantro leaves

2 tablespoons ghee or butter, melted

1 Sift the flour, sugar, salt, and baking powder into a large bowl. Whisk the egg and milk together, then gradually add to the flour mixture and stir until a dough is formed.

2 Transfer the dough to a work surface, make a depression in the center of the dough, and add the oil. Knead for 3–4 minutes, until you have a smooth and pliable dough. Wrap the dough in plastic wrap and let rest for 1 hour.

3 Divide the dough into eight equal pieces, form each piece into a ball, and flatten into a thick cake. Cover with plastic wrap and let rest for 10–15 minutes.

4 Preheat the broiler to high, line a broiler pan with aluminum foil, and brush with oil. Roll each flattened cake into a 5-inch circle and pull the lower end gently. Carefully roll out again, maintaining the teardrop shape, until about 9 inches long.

5 Mix the chiles and cilantro together, then spread over the surface of the naans. Press gently so that the mixture sticks to the dough. Transfer a naan to the prepared broiler pan and cook until slightly puffed and brown. Turn over and cook the other side, until lightly browned. Remove from the broiler and brush with the melted ghee. Wrap in a dish towel while you cook the remaining naans.

Chapattis
CHAPATIS

In Indian homes, chapatis are made fresh every day, using a special flour known as *atta*. Asian grocery stores sell atta, but you can replace it with 1½ cups whole-wheat flour sifted with 1½ cups all-purpose flour.

MAKES: 16

PREP: 20 minutes, plus resting time

COOK: 25–30 minutes

3 cups chapati flour (atta), plus extra for dusting

1 teaspoon salt

½ teaspoon sugar

2 tablespoons vegetable oil or peanut oil

1 cup lukewarm water

1 Mix the chapati flour, salt, and sugar together in a large bowl. Add the oil and work well into the flour mixture with your fingertips. Gradually add the water, mixing at the same time. When a dough is formed, transfer it to a work surface and knead for 4–5 minutes, or until all the excess moisture has been absorbed by the flour. Wrap the dough in plastic wrap and let rest for 30 minutes.

2 Divide the dough in half, then cut each half into eight equal pieces. Form each piece into a ball and flatten into a round cake. Dust each cake lightly with flour and roll out to a 6-inch circle. Keep the remaining cakes covered while you are working on one. The chapatis will cook better when freshly rolled out, so roll out and cook one at a time.

3 Preheat a heavy, cast-iron griddle or a large, heavy skillet over medium–high heat. Put a chapati on the griddle and cook for 30 seconds. Using a spatula, turn over and cook until bubbles begin to appear on the surface. Turn over again. Press the edges down gently with a clean cloth to encourage the chapati to puff up—they will not always puff up, but this doesn't matter. Cook until brown patches appear on the underside. Remove from the griddle and keep hot by wrapping in a piece of aluminum foil lined with paper towels. Repeat until all the chapatis have been cooked.

Poori

POORIS

These deep-fried breads puff up to look like balloons when they go into the hot oil. Children love watching them being cooked, but always keep them a safe distance away. Pooris are perfect for serving with most Indian dishes.

MAKES: 12

PREP: 20–25 minutes, plus resting time

COOK: 20–25 minutes

2 cups whole-wheat flour, sifted, plus extra for dusting

½ teaspoon salt

2 tablespoons ghee or butter, melted

½–¾ cup cold water

vegetable oil or peanut oil, for deep-frying

1 Put the flour and salt into a bowl and drizzle the ghee over the surface. Gradually stir in the water until a stiff dough forms. Turn out the dough onto a lightly floured surface and knead for 10 minutes, or until it is smooth and elastic. Shape the dough into a ball and place it in a clean bowl, then cover with a damp dish towel and let rest for 20 minutes.

2 Divide the dough into 12 equal pieces and roll each into a ball. Flatten each ball of dough between your palms, then thinly roll it out on a lightly floured surface into a 5-inch circle. Continue until all the dough balls have been rolled out.

3 Heat enough oil for deep frying in a large saucepan or deep fryer to 350–375°F, or until a cube of bread browns in 30 seconds. Drop a poori into the hot oil and fry for about 10 seconds, or until it puffs up. Use two large spoons to flip the poori over and spoon some hot oil over the top.

4 Use the spoons to lift the poori from the oil and let any excess oil drip back into the pan. Drain the poori on paper towels and serve immediately. Continue cooking until all the pooris have been fried, making sure the oil returns to the correct temperature before you add the next poori.

Besan ki roti

SPICED CHICKPEA FLOUR FLATBREADS

These tasty flatbreads are prepared using a mixture of chickpea flour (also called besan flour or gram flour)—which is made from ground chickpeas—and whole-wheat. They are nutritious, high in protein, and delicious served warm with any vegetable, lentil, or chicken curry.

MAKES: 8

PREP: 20 minutes, plus resting time

COOK: 25–30 minutes

1 cup whole-wheat flour

1¼ cups chickpea (besan) flour, plus extra for dusting

2 teaspoons salt

2 tablespoons finely chopped fresh cilantro

2 fresh red chiles, finely chopped

2 teaspoons cumin seeds

1 teaspoon crushed coriander seeds

1 teaspoon ground turmeric

5 tablespoons ghee or butter, melted, plus extra for brushing

1 cup cold water

1 Sift the flours and salt into a large mixing bowl, adding the bran left in the bottom of the sifter. Add all the remaining ingredients except the water. Mix together and gradually add the water to form a soft, pliable dough. Knead on a lightly floured surface for 1–2 minutes, then let rest for 10 minutes.

2 Divide the dough into eight equal balls, then roll out each one into a 4½–6-inch circle. Brush the top of each with a little extra melted ghee.

3 Heat a nonstick, cast-iron griddle or heavy skillet over medium heat. When hot, cook the dough circles, one at a time, for 1–2 minutes on each side, pressing down with a spatula. Remove from the griddle, transfer to a plate, and cover with aluminum foil to keep warm while you cook the remaining flatbreads. Serve warm.

TIP

For a less spicy version of these flatbreads, simply omit the chile from this recipe.

PARATHAS

Parathas are pan-fried, unleavened breads that are often prepared for special occasions and religious festivals. Made with plenty of melted ghee, parathas have a flaky texture and are too rich for everyday meals—unless you don't worry about your waistline. For an Indian-style breakfast, try them with a bowl of yogurt.

MAKES: 8

PREP: 30 minutes, plus resting time

COOK: 25–30 minutes

2 cups whole-wheat flour, sifted, plus extra for dusting

½ teaspoon salt

⅔–1 cup cold water

⅔ cup ghee or 1¼ sticks butter, melted

1 Mix the flour and salt together in a large bowl and make a well in the center. Gradually stir in enough of the water to make a stiff dough. Turn out the dough onto a lightly floured surface and knead for 10 minutes, or until smooth and elastic. Shape the dough into a ball and place in a large bowl, then cover with a damp dish towel and let rest for 20 minutes.

2 Divide the dough into eight equal pieces. Lightly flour your hands and roll each piece of dough into a ball. Working with one ball of dough at a time, roll it out on a lightly floured surface to a form a 5-inch circle. Brush the top of the dough with 1½ teaspoons of the melted ghee. Fold the circle in half to make a semicircular shape and brush the top again with melted ghee. Fold the semicircular shape in half again to make a triangular shape. Press the layers together.

3 Roll out the triangle on a lightly floured surface into a larger triangle about 7 inches on each side. Flip the dough back and forth between your hands a couple of times, then cover with a damp dish towel and continue until all the dough is shaped and rolled.

4 Meanwhile, heat a large, dry skillet or cast-iron griddle over high heat until hot and a splash of water "dances" when it hits the surface. Place a paratha in the pan and cook until bubbles appear on the surface. Flip the paratha over and brush the surface with melted ghee. Continue cooking until the bottom is golden brown, then flip the paratha over again and smear with more melted ghee. Use a spatula to press down on the surface of the paratha so it cooks evenly.

5 Brush with more melted ghee and serve immediately, then repeat with the remaining parathas. Parathas are best served as soon as they come out of the pan, but they can be kept warm wrapped in aluminum foil for about 20 minutes.

Aloo gobhi parathas

PARATHAS STUFFED WITH POTATO & CAULIFLOWER

These tasty flatbreads are stuffed with a spicy potato-and-cauliflower mixture before being rolled again and cooked in the usual way. They are delicious eaten with a bowl of yogurt or a raita and pickle, and can be served as an accompaniment to any main dish.

MAKES: 8

PREP: 30 minutes, plus resting time

COOK: 35–40 minutes

2 cups whole-wheat flour

¾ cup all-purpose flour, plus extra for dusting

1 teaspoon freshly ground cardamom seeds

2 teaspoons salt

1 cup warm buttermilk

⅔ cup ghee or 1¼ sticks butter, melted

FILLING

2 tablespoons vegetable oil or peanut oil

2 teaspoons cumin seeds

1 tablespoon hot curry powder

4 garlic cloves, crushed

2 teaspoons finely grated fresh ginger

1 cup finely chopped cauliflower florets

2 teaspoons salt

2 russet or Yukon gold potatoes, boiled, peeled, and coarsely mashed

⅓ cup finely chopped fresh cilantro

1 First, make the filling. Heat the oil in a large skillet over medium heat. Add the cumin seeds, curry powder, garlic, ginger, and cauliflower and sauté for 8–10 minutes, or until the cauliflower has softened. Add the salt and the mashed potatoes and stir well to mix evenly. Remove from the heat and stir in the chopped cilantro. Let cool.

2 Sift together the flours, ground cardamom seeds, and salt into a large bowl, adding the bran left in the bottom of the sifter. Make a well in the center and pour in the buttermilk and 2 tablespoons of the melted ghee. Work into the flour mixture to make a soft dough. Knead on a lightly floured surface for 10 minutes and form into a ball. Put the dough into a large bowl, cover with a damp cloth, and let rest for 20 minutes. Divide the dough into eight equal balls, then roll out each into a 6-inch circle.

3 Place a little of the filling into the center of each dough circle and fold up the edges into the center to enclose the filling. Press down lightly and, using a lightly floured rolling pin, roll out to make a 6-inch paratha. Repeat with the remaining dough and filling.

4 Heat a nonstick, flat, cast-iron griddle or heavy skillet over medium heat. Brush each paratha with a little of the remaining melted ghee. Brush the griddle with a little melted ghee. Put a paratha in the griddle and cook for 1–2 minutes, pressing down with a spatula. Turn over, brush with a little more ghee, and cook for an additional 1–2 minutes, or until flecked with light-brown spots. Remove from the griddle, transfer to a plate, and cover with aluminum foil to keep warm while you cook the remaining parathas. Serve warm.

CHAPTER 6
DESSERTS
& DRINKS

Aam ki kulfi

MANGO KULFI

Kulfi is a dairy-based dessert flavored with fruits and nuts, in this case mangoes and pistachio nuts. Traditionally, it is made by reducing a large volume of milk to the consistency of condensed milk. This recipe is less labor-intensive, using evaporated milk and cream.

SERVES: 6

PREP: 5–10 minutes, plus cooling & chilling time

COOK: 10–15 minutes

1 (12-fluid-ounce) can evaporated milk

1¼ cups light cream

¼ cup ground almonds (almond meal)

½–⅔ cup sugar, to taste

2 mangoes, peeled, pitted, and coarsely chopped, then the flesh pureed in a food processor

1 teaspoon freshly ground cardamom seeds

3 tablespoons shelled, unsalted pistachio nuts, to decorate

1 Pour the evaporated milk and cream into a heavy saucepan and stir to mix. Place over medium heat. Mix the ground almonds and sugar together, then add to the evaporated milk mixture. Cook, stirring, for 6–8 minutes, until the mixture thickens slightly.

2 Remove from the heat and let the mixture cool completely, stirring from time to time to prevent a skin from forming. When completely cold, stir in the mango puree and ground cardamom.

3 Meanwhile, preheat a small saucepan over medium heat, add the pistachio nuts, and toast for 2–3 minutes. Let cool, then lightly crush. Store in an airtight container until required.

4 Fill six kulfi molds with the mango mixture and freeze for 5–6 hours. Before serving, transfer to the refrigerator for 40 minutes, then invert onto serving plates. Serve sprinkled with the crushed pistachio nuts to decorate.

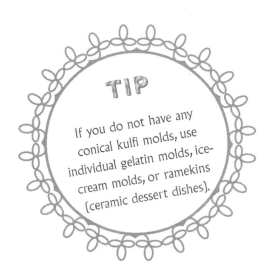

TIP

If you do not have any conical kulfi molds, use individual gelatin molds, ice-cream molds, or ramekins (ceramic dessert dishes).

Gajar ka halwa

SOFT CARROT FUDGE

This delicious dessert is made by cooking shredded carrots in thickened milk to a soft, fudge-like consistency. A variety of contrasts in taste and texture is created by adding raisins, mixed nuts, cardamom, nutmeg, and rose water.

SERVES: 4–6

¼ cup ghee or 4 tablespoons unsalted butter

1-inch piece cinnamon stick, halved

¼ cup slivered almonds

3 tablespoons cashew nuts

2 tablespoons raisins

4 cups shredded carrots

2½ cups milk

⅔ cup sugar

½ teaspoon freshly ground cardamom seeds

½ teaspoon freshly grated nutmeg

¼ cup heavy cream

2 tablespoons rose water

vanilla ice cream or whipped cream, to serve

PREP: 15 minutes, plus cooling time

1 Melt the ghee in a heavy saucepan over low heat. Add the cinnamon stick and let sizzle gently for 25–30 seconds. Add the slivered almonds and cashew nuts and cook, stirring, until lightly browned. Remove about 2 teaspoons of the nuts and set aside.

2 Add the raisins, carrots, milk, and sugar to the saucepan, increase the heat to medium, and bring the milk to boiling point. Continue to cook over low–medium heat for 15–20 minutes, until the milk evaporates completely, stirring frequently and blending in any thickened milk that sticks to the side of the saucepan. Don't let any milk that is stuck to the side brown or burn, because this will give the dessert an unpleasant flavor.

COOK: 20–25 minutes

3 Stir in the ground cardamom, nutmeg, cream, and rose water. Remove from the heat and let cool slightly, then serve immediately topped with a scoop of ice cream or a dollop of whipped cream. Sprinkle the reserved nuts on top to decorate.

Firni

INDIAN RICE DESSERT

This is a immensely popular north Indian dessert, where rice flour is cooked in thickened milk with apricots, raisins, almonds, and pistachios with the exotic aromas of rose water and cardamom. It is best served chilled.

SERVES: 4

PREP: 10–15 minutes, plus cooling & chilling time

COOK: 20–25 minutes

good pinch of saffron threads, pounded

2 tablespoons hot milk

3 tablespoons ghee or unsalted butter

⅓ cup rice flour

¼ cup slivered almonds

2 tablespoons raisins

2½ cups regular whole milk

1¾ cups evaporated milk

¼ cup sugar

12 dried apricots, sliced

1 teaspoon freshly ground cardamom seeds

½ teaspoon freshly grated nutmeg

2 tablespoons rose water

TO DECORATE

¼ cup walnut pieces

2 tablespoons shelled, unsalted pistachio nuts

1 Put the pounded saffron in the hot milk and let soak until needed. Reserve 2 teaspoons of the ghee and melt the remainder in a heavy saucepan over low heat. Add the rice flour, slivered almonds, and raisins and cook, stirring, for 2 minutes. Add the milk, increase the heat to medium, and cook, stirring, until it begins to bubble gently. Reduce the heat to low and cook for 10–12 minutes, stirring frequently to prevent the mixture from sticking to the pan.

2 Add the evaporated milk, sugar, and apricots, reserving a few slices to decorate. Cook, stirring, until the mixture thickens to the consistency of a white sauce.

3 Add the reserved saffron-and-milk mixture, the ground cardamom, nutmeg, and rose water, stir to distribute well, and remove from the heat. Let cool, then cover and chill in the refrigerator for at least 2 hours.

4 Melt the reserved ghee in a small saucepan over low heat. Add the walnut pieces and cook, stirring, until they brown a little. Remove and drain on paper towels. Brown the pistachio nuts in the saucepan, remove, and drain on paper towels. Let the pistachio nuts cool, then lightly crush.

5 Serve the dessert decorated with the fried nuts and the reserved apricot slices.

Dudh pak

CREAMY ALMOND, PISTACHIO & RICE PUDDING

There are many different versions of this creamy milk-and-rice pudding, which is originally from Gujarat. This version is scented with cardamom and flavored with pistachios and almonds. It needs constant stirring, but is well worth the effort.

SERVES: 4

PREP: 5 minutes, plus resting time

COOK: 25–30 minutes, plus standing time

8½ cups milk

¼ cup basmati rice

½ cup sugar

1 teaspoon freshly ground cardamom seeds

⅓ cup finely chopped pistachio nuts

⅓ cup finely chopped blanched almonds

1 Pour the milk into a large, heavy saucepan and bring to a boil.

2 Add the rice and cook over medium heat, stirring constantly, for 18–20 minutes, or until the rice is tender.

3 Add the sugar, stir, and cook for an additional 3–4 minutes.

4 Remove from the heat and stir in the ground cardamom and the nuts. Cover and let stand for 20 minutes before serving.

TIP

This dessert is usually eaten warm, but it is equally delicious served chilled.

Malai khumani

MIXED NUT & DRIED FRUIT DESSERTS

This sweet and creamy dessert originates from the royal state of Hyderabad in south India. The decoration of edible silver or gold leaf (*varak*) is optional, but it transforms this simple dessert into one worthy of any celebration, whether it is a wedding, birthday, or religious festival.

SERVES: 4

PREP: 20 minutes, plus soaking & chilling time

COOK: 0 minutes

1½ cups dried apricots

⅔ cup gold raisins

½ cup orange juice

1¼ cups heavy cream

¼ cup sugar

1 teaspoon rose water

¼ cup finely chopped pistachio nuts

¼ cup finely chopped walnuts

¼ cup finely chopped hazelnuts

edible silver or gold leaf, to decorate (optional)

1 Coarsely chop the apricots and put into a bowl with the golden raisins and orange juice. Cover and let soak for 20 minutes.

2 In a separate bowl, whisk the cream, sugar, and rose water until the cream holds soft peaks. Gently fold in the chopped nuts.

3 Divide the reserved apricot mixture among four dessert glasses. Spoon the cream mixture over it and chill in the refrigerator for 3–4 hours.

4 Decorate each dessert with edible silver or gold leaf, if using, and serve immediately.

TIP

To use the silver or gold leaf, put the shiny side on the dessert, with the paper backing facing up, and use a paintbrush to dab on the paper side. The silver will transfer to the dessert.

Kheer

RICE PUDDING WITH CARDAMOM & PISTACHIOS

This rich, creamy dessert from northern India can be made to be thick or very liquid with the rice floating in the milk, depending on your personal preference. This lightly spiced version is delicious served with fresh fruit.

SERVES: 4–6

PREP: 5 minutes, plus soaking & chilling time

COOK: 1¼–1½ hours

½ cup basmati rice

5 cups milk, plus extra to taste

seeds from 4 green cardamom pods

1 cinnamon stick

½ cup superfine or granulated sugar, or to taste

TO SERVE

grated palm sugar or light brown sugar

chopped toasted pistachio nuts

1 Wash the rice in several changes of water until the water runs clear, then let soak in a bowl of fresh cold water for 30 minutes. Drain and set aside until ready to cook.

2 Rinse a saucepan with water and do not dry. Pour the milk into the pan, add the cardamom seeds and cinnamon stick, and stir in the rice and superfine sugar.

3 Put the pan over medium–high heat and slowly bring to a boil, stirring. Reduce the heat to its lowest setting and let the mixture simmer, stirring frequently, for about 1 hour, until the rice is tender and the mixture has thickened. When the rice is tender, you can stir in extra milk if you prefer the pudding with a soupier texture, or continue simmering if you prefer it thicker.

4 Serve hot or transfer to a bowl and let cool completely, stirring frequently, then cover and chill. When ready to serve, spoon into individual bowls and sprinkle with the palm sugar and pistachio nuts.

Shrikhand anaari

SAFFRON YOGURT WITH POMEGRANATE

This is the west Indian way of transforming everyday yogurt into a luscious dessert. In Maharashtra, *shrikhand* is traditionally served with hot pooris, straight from the pan, but fresh fruit also makes a tasty accompaniment.

SERVES: 4

PREP: 10–15 minutes, plus draining & chilling

COOK: 5 minutes, plus infusing time

4½ cups plain yogurt
¼ teaspoon saffron threads
2 tablespoons milk
¼ cup sugar, or to taste
seeds from 2 green cardamom pods
2 pomegranates

1 Line a strainer set over a bowl with a piece of cheesecloth large enough to hang over the edges. Add the yogurt, then tie the corners of the cheesecloth into a tight knot and tie them to the kitchen faucet. Let the bundle hang over the sink for 4 hours, or until the excess moisture has dripped away.

2 Put the saffron threads in a dry saucepan over high heat and toast, stirring frequently, until you can smell the aroma. Immediately remove them from the pan.

3 Put the milk into the pan, return the saffron threads, and warm until bubbles appear around the edge, then set aside and let steep.

4 When the yogurt is thick and creamy, put it into a bowl, stir in the sugar, cardamom seeds, and saffron-and-milk mixture, and beat until smooth. Taste and add extra sugar, if desired. Cover and chill for at least 1 hour, until well chilled.

5 Meanwhile, to prepare the pomegranates, cut each in half and use your fingers to scoop out the seeds.

6 To serve, spoon the yogurt mixture into individual bowls and sprinkle with the pomegranate seeds.

TIP
For an everyday family dessert, omit the saffron threads and cardamom seeds. Flavor with ground ginger and cinnamon and add sugar to taste.

Mishti doi

BENGALI CARAMEL YOGURT

Traditionally set in earthenware pots, this sweetened yogurt dish is the quintessential dessert, without which a Bengali meal cannot be complete. You can add a small pinch of saffron threads to flavor the milk mixture, if desired.

SERVES: 4

PREP: 5 minutes, plus chilling time

COOK: 20 minutes, plus standing time

1½ cups evaporated milk
⅔ cup condensed milk
2 tablespoons sugar
½ cup plain yogurt, whisked

1 Pour the evaporated milk and condensed milk into a saucepan over medium heat and bring to a boil. Reduce the heat to low, stir, and simmer gently for 10 minutes, or until well combined. Remove from the heat.

2 Meanwhile, in a separate small saucepan, heat the sugar over low heat until it starts to melt, turns golden, and begins to caramelize. Remove from the heat.

3 Add the caramelized sugar to the milk mixture and stir to mix well. When the milk mixture is just warm, stir in the yogurt and mix well.

4 Pour the mixture into four small serving bowls, cover with plastic wrap, and let stand in a warm place for 8–10 hours or overnight, until lightly set. Transfer to the refrigerator and chill for 4–6 hours before serving.

TIP
You can add a teaspoon of ground cardamom seeds to the milk mixture for a spicier flavor, if desired.

Bebinca

GOAN LAYERED COCONUT CAKE

This rich Goan dessert has its influence from the Portuguese, who ruled Goa from the sixteenth century until its liberation in 1961. It is a dense, moist cake that is traditionally cooked layer by layer over hot coals. It is time-consuming to make, but the result is well worth the effort. It is delicious served cold with vanilla ice cream.

SERVES: 8–10

PREP: 15 minutes, plus chilling time

COOK: 1¾–2 hours

1¾ cups coconut milk

1½ cups sugar

10 egg yolks, lightly beaten

1⅔ cups all-purpose flour

½ teaspoon freshly grated nutmeg

1 teaspoon freshly ground cardamom seeds

pinch of ground cloves

¼ teaspoon ground cinnamon

1 stick butter, plus extra for greasing

1 Preheat the oven to 400°F. Lightly grease a 6½-inch nonstick, round cake pan and line with parchment paper.

2 Pour the coconut milk into a saucepan and stir in the sugar. Heat gently for 8–10 minutes, stirring until the sugar has dissolved. Remove from the heat and gradually add the beaten egg yolks, whisking all the time so that the eggs do not scramble and the mixture is smooth. Sift in the flour and spices and stir to make a smooth batter.

3 Melt the butter, then add a tablespoon to the prepared cake pan and spread it over the bottom. Pour one-eighth of the batter into the pan and spread to coat the bottom evenly. Bake in the preheated oven for 10–12 minutes, or until set.

4 Remove from the oven and brush another spoonful of the melted butter over the top, followed by another eighth of the batter. Return to the oven and cook for 10–12 minutes, or until set.

5 Repeat this process until all the butter and batter has been used, baking the last layer for an additional 20–25 minutes, or until the top is golden brown and the cake is firmly set. Remove from the oven and let cool in the pan.

6 When cool, remove the cake from the pan, cover with plastic wrap, and chill for 4–6 hours before serving.

Masala chai

MASALA TEA

There is always time for a cup of tea, or *chai*. Many offices in India have a *chai walla*, and vendors sell it freshly brewed on street corners and train platforms. This milky version is drunk all over India.

SERVES: 4

PREP: 5 minutes

COOK: 15 minutes, plus steeping time

4 cups cold water

1-inch piece fresh ginger, coarsely chopped

1 cinnamon stick

3 green cardamom pods, crushed

3 cloves

1½ tablespoons Assam tea leaves

sugar and milk, to taste

1 Pour the water into a heavy saucepan over medium–high heat. Add the ginger, cinnamon stick, cardamom pods, and cloves and bring to a boil. Reduce the heat and simmer for 10 minutes.

2 Put the tea leaves into a teapot and pour in the water and spices. Stir and let steep for 5 minutes.

3 Strain the tea into four teacups or heatproof glasses and add sugar and milk to taste.

TIP

For iced masala tea, allow the tea to cool completely in step 2, then strain into a jug and chill. Serve in tall glasses with ice, sugar and lemon wedges.

Namkeen lassi

SALT LASSI

"Salt lassi or sweet lassi?" This is the question anyone in India has to answer over and over. This chilled yogurt drink is universally popular and served everywhere, from the grandest hotels to the most humble beachside shacks.

SERVES: 4   **PREP:** 5 minutes   **COOK:** 0 minutes

3 cups plain yogurt
½ teaspoon salt
¼ teaspoon sugar
1 cup cold water
ice cubes, to serve
ground cumin and fresh mint sprigs, to decorate

1 Beat together the yogurt, salt, and sugar in a bowl, then add the water and whisk until frothy.

2 Fill four glasses with ice cubes and pour the yogurt mixture over them. Lightly dust with cumin and top with mint sprigs to decorate.

TIP

For a sweet lassi, add ¼ cup of sugar and omit the salt. You can decorate with ground cumin and finely chopped toasted pistachios.

Falooda

ROSE & VERMICELLI MILK SHAKE

Falooda is popular not just in Mumbai, where it is thought to have originated, but also in the rest of the country. This chilled drink/dessert is the perfect way to cool off in the summer heat. *Tukmaria*, or basil seeds (available online), used in this recipe, have a mild flavor (somewhat like poppy seeds) and are generally used in light desserts.

SERVES: 4

PREP: 20 minutes, plus soaking time

COOK: 5–10 minutes

2 teaspoons edible basil seeds (tukmaria)

1 cup cold water

¼ ounce fine rice vermicelli (sevai)

½ cup rose syrup

4 cups chilled milk

4 scoops of vanilla ice cream

1 Put the basil seeds into a bowl and pour the water over them. Let soak for 15 minutes, or until swollen and gelatin-like. Drain and set aside.

2 Meanwhile, break the vermicelli into small pieces and cook according to the package directions. Drain and refresh under cold running water.

3 To assemble the drinks, pour the rose syrup into the bottoms of four glasses. Divide the soaked basil seeds and the drained vermicelli among the glasses.

4 Pour the chilled milk over the seeds and vermicelli and top each with a scoop of ice cream. Serve immediately.

TIP
For a mango falooda, replace the rose syrup with mango puree.